SPAIN

POCKET GUIDE

Walking Eye
mobile app

Discover the world's best destinations with the Insight Guides Walking Eye app, available to download for free in the App Store and Google Play.

The container app provides easy access to fantastic free content on events and activities taking place in your current location or chosen destination, with the possibility of booking, as well as the regularly-updated Insight Guides travel blog: Inspire Me. In addition, you can purchase curated, premium destination guides through the app, which feature local highlights, hotel, bar, restaurant and shopping listings, an A to Z of practical information and more. Or purchase and download Insight Guides eBooks straight to your device.

INSIGHT GUIDES

Walking Eye

○ **DESTINATIONS**

○ **INSPIRE ME**

○ **EBOOKS**

○ **EVENTS**

TOP 10 ATTRACTIONS

LA MEZQUITA, CÓRDOBA
A stunning example of Moorish architectural prowess. See page 57.

SEVILLE'S CATHEDRAL
Its landmark Giralda tower is the world's largest Gothic church. See page 54.

BARCELONA
Home to Gaudí's eccentric Sagrada Família church. See page 44.

THE COSTAS
From rocky coves to sandy beaches, each coast has its own distinctive character. See page 65.

THE PICOS DE EUROPA
These mountains provide some of the most dramatic scenery in Spain. See page 86.

THE ALHAMBRA, GRANADA
The grandest of all monuments left by the Moors. See page 59.

THE MUSEO DEL PRADO
With its art treasures, this is one of the top attractions of Madrid. See page 32.

MUSEO GUGGENHEIM, BILBAO
The futuristic museum is the top attraction of the Basque Country. See page 96.

SALVADOR DALÍ
His works feature prominently on the Costa Brava. See page 66.

TOLEDO
Spectacularly situated on the River Tajo, it's famous for its cathedral and the works of El Greco. See page 35.

A PERFECT DAY

9.00am

La Rambla
Get an early start on Barcelona's La Rambla, to enjoy it before the crowds arrive. Pick up your newspaper from a newsstand then pop into La Boqueria market – at its most colourful in the morning – for a proper Catalan breakfast of baby squid and poached eggs.

1.30pm

Lunchtime
Get into the local rhythm and have a *menú del dia*, three courses at remarkably low rates in a neighbourhood bar like Rodrigo in Argentería, or around the Passeig del Born. Another option is to walk 10 minutes to Barceloneta for a paella by the sea at Can Majó.

10.30am

Gothic Quarter
Across La Rambla is the Gothic Quarter. Meander through its shady, narrow lanes and palm-filled courtyards. Get the background on today's Old Town at the City History Museum (MUHAB) or have a coffee break in the diminutive Meson del Café on Llibretería.

12 noon

Breathtaking church
Over Via Laietana is the Born district. Glimpse the breathtaking interior of Santa Maria del Mar, or sip *una copa de cava* on the terrace of La Vinya del Senyor and admire the church facade.

3.30pm

Siesta break

A gentle stroll along the Passeig Marítim towards the Vila Olímpica, pausing for coffee in one of the waterfront *xiringuitos* (beach bars), is ideal for working off lunch. Indulge in a taxi back to base for a reviving siesta, essential to keep up the pace until the wee hours.

8.30pm

Drinks and *tapas*

Relax at one of the many terrace bars in elegant Rambla Catalunya, or try the eponymous cocktail at Dry Martini, Aribau 162. Afterwards go for *tapas*, the perfect dinner, especially when created by top chef Carles Abellan at Tapas 24.

11.00pm

On the town

Round off the day in style just up the road at designer Club Ommsession, Rosselló 265, part of award-winning Hotel Omm, where you can rub shoulders with the sleek and beautiful. Alternatively, catch a cab to Mirablau, halfway up Tibidabo hill, and dance till dawn overlooking the city.

5.30pm

Explore the Eixample

A session of retail therapy in the *modernista* setting of the Eixample is recommended for all the family. Those who don't shop can visit a Gaudí building, like La Pedrera or Casa Batlló, or just wander around the area to see a wealth of decorative details, from stained glass to ceramics, by his genius contemporaries.

CONTENTS

INTRODUCTION

Spain is located in the far southwest of Europe and comprises the largest part of the Iberian Peninsula (with Portugal claiming a narrow strip hugging most of the western coastline). The Balearic Islands of Ibiza, Mallorca and Menorca, in the western Mediterranean, also belong to Spain, as do the sub-tropical Canary Islands, off the west coast of Africa.

EVOLUTION OF MODERN SPAIN

Starting with the Phoenicians' founding of Cádiz in 1100BC, Spain was colonised over a period of some 2,500 years by such diverse cultures as the Carthaginians, Romans, Vandals, Visigoths and the Moors, all of whom contributed to the character of the country. It was not until the Catholic Monarchs, Fernando (Ferdinand) and Isabel, drove the last remaining Moors from their capital in Granada in 1492 that Spain became a united country. At the same time, the relationship between Catholics and people of Jewish and Moorish origin was marred by the Spanish Inquisition, which persecuted the latter two groups and expelled them from the country. The same year saw the event that started Spain's Golden Age – the first modern European voyage to America led to Spain becoming

Tiled mural inside Valencia's railway station

fabulously wealthy from her Southern American colonies. These treasures, however, were soon squandered in pointless wars and Spain retreated, introspectively, behind the formidable barrier of the Pyrenees mountains.

Wide open spaces

While Spain is (at 504,880 sq km/194,885 sq miles) the third largest country in Europe, after Russia and France, it has a proportionately small population (just 46.5 million). Consequently, and unusually in Europe, vast areas of the country remain wild, rugged and under-populated.

It was a desperately poor Spain that re-emerged onto the international stage in 1936, torn asunder in a violent civil war between the left-leaning Republicans – assisted by the famed International Brigades – and the right-wing Nationalists led by General Franco, helped by German and Italian military might. After his victory in 1939, Franco instituted a harsh dictatorship that ended only with his death in 1975. He was succeeded as head of state by King Juan Carlos I who, despite having been groomed as a successor by Franco, surprised the country by setting in motion a rapid and bloodless transformation of Spain into a democratic constitutional monarchy. Since then, general elections have seen the government controlled by parties of both the left and of the right. During the past two decades, more and more power has devolved to the 17 autonomous regions.

REGIONAL PRIDE

Spain's varied terrain and the assimilation of so many diverse cultures have shaped the character of its peoples. And it is, in reality, peoples in the plural. Some of the country's 17 autonomous regions are fiercely independent – both in their thinking and in their relative freedom from interference by central government, a combination that has given rise to passionate 'regional nationalism', most notably among the Catalans and Basques, but in other regions as well. This is reflected in the use of local languages rather than Castilian Spanish. In fact, only about 60 percent of Spaniards use Castilian as their first language.

Despite the regions differing widely in custom and character, they generally share a very 'Spanish' lifestyle. This includes a love of children, devotion to family and friends, and an open and inclusive social life that involves partaking of much food and wine.

RICH SCENIC DIVERSITY

Impressive mountain ranges, such as the Pyrenees and Sierra Nevada, as well as lesser-known massifs, are spread throughout Spain's mainland, which is largely made up of the central plateau, or *meseta*. And, not to be outdone, the Canary Island of Tenerife has Mt Teide – the highest peak in the country. Along Spain's Atlantic and Mediterranean coasts – and, of course, on the islands – you find almost every conceivable type of beach environment. Inland are powerful rivers, arid plateaux, wide plains and even, in Almería and on the island of Fuerteventura, desert.

Madrid is the Spanish capital and transport hub, located at the geographical heart of the country, and is the most obvious place to start. Not only is it of importance in its own right, but it can also be used as a base to visit a host of fascinating nearby sights. **Barcelona**, world famous for its architecture and style, is a must-see. In fact, if anything, it has more individual attractions than Madrid. **Andalucía**, a name evocative of passionate emotion, is also a highlight, with its famous white villages and spectacular Moorish heritage in the cities of **Seville**, **Córdoba** and **Granada**.

Millions of people visit Spain each year with the aim of simply relaxing on a beach, and they are spoilt for choice. The famous **Costas** stretch from the Costa Brava at the eastern end of the Pyrenees all the way round past Gibraltar to the Costa de la Luz and the border with Portugal. Less well known is the **Costa Verde** (Green Coast), which is different in almost all respects from the

Modernisme in Barcelona

other Costas, and stretches along the northern coast, passing through Cantabria, Asturias and Galicia on its way from the Basque Country. Don't forget, either, the **Balearic Islands** off Spain's eastern Mediterranean coast, with resorts ranging from the rowdy to the refined. Visitors in search of serious winter sunshine need look no further than the volcanic **Canary Islands**. Just off the coast of northwest Africa, these seven islands are very different in character.

Spain also has a score of less-travelled places. The **Basque Country**, an entity unto itself, is graced by the elegant town of **San Sebastián** and by the stylish city of **Bilbao**, home to the Guggenheim Museum. Ancient **Castilla y León** has the fine old Castilian cities of **Burgos**, **León**, **Salamanca** and **Segovia**. **Navarra** is renowned for the bull-running in **Pamplona**, but also has beautiful green countryside. **La Rioja** is justly famous for its wines, and the old kingdom of **Aragón** stretches from the high Pyrenees down to its capital **Zaragoza** and on to **Teruel**. Between Madrid and Andalucía are two of the least-visited regions of Spain: **Castilla-La Mancha** is well known for its wines and Don Quixote windmills, and the isolated city of **Cuenca** is famed for its Casas Colgadas (Hanging Houses). **Extremadura** has always been remote, but that didn't stop the Romans from making **Mérida** one of its major towns. **Cáceres**, also Roman, is important for its 16th-century palaces.

A BRIEF HISTORY

Spain's history is as rugged and colourful as the land itself. It is a tale of Roman and Moorish domination and a glorious Golden Age; of empires and colonies conquered and defeated; of brave knights and foolish kings; and of a bloody and destructive civil war that saw Spain cut off from the international community for some four decades of the 20th century. Since Franco's death in 1975, Spain's transformation into a modern European state has been nothing short of spectacular.

EARLY INFLUENCES

The earliest inhabitants of the Iberian Peninsula were Paleolithic people who probably arrived via a land bridge linking Europe and Africa between Gibraltar and Morocco. As the Ice Age gripped Europe, the first Iberians put on bearskin coats, stoked up their fires, and fed off deer, bison and wild horses – just like those depicted on the walls and ceilings of caves discovered in Cantabria, near Altamira, which date back at least 15,000 years.

During the Bronze Age, Celtic migrants settled in northern and central Spain, while the south and east were inhabited by various Iberian tribes of North African origin. The Iberians had their own written language, sophisticated industry and tools, and they created fine works of art, such as the stone sculpture of a female deity, known as *La Dama de Elche* (The Lady of Elche), a star attraction at Madrid's Archaeological Museum. The Celts and the Iberians interacted where their territories overlapped and developed a distinct Celtiberian culture. The Celtiberians soon gained fame as warriors and it is said that they invented the two-edged sword, later to become standard equipment in the Roman army, and to be used against their inventors.

Before this, Phoenicians, sailing from bases in North Africa, founded several colonies in southern Spain. The first of these, established in about 1100BC, was Gadir (present-day Cádiz). Carthage, which was itself a Phoenician colony, established an empire of its own that spread as far north into Spain as Barcelona and the island of Mallorca. Barcelona was the base from which Carthaginian forces under Hannibal set out to defeat Rome in the 3rd century BC, nearly succeeding in their objective before being defeated by the Romans in the Second Punic War. The defeat

Tarragona's Roman aqueduct, Pont del Diable

of the Carthaginians left the way open for Rome to take control of the peninsula, though it took nearly 200 years to subjugate the stubbornly resistant Celtiberians.

SPAIN UNDER THE CAESARS

Second only to the homeland itself, Spain was to become the most important part of the Roman Empire. In many parts of the country the stamp of Roman civilisation remains: in roads and bridges, walls and vineyards, as well as in the ruins of aqueducts and amphitheatres, palaces and villas. Three living Spanish languages are descended from Latin: Gallego (Galician), Castilian (Spanish) and Catalan. Roman law forms the foundation of the Spanish legal system, and Spain gave birth to Roman emperors as memorable as Trajan and Hadrian, as well as the writers Seneca and Martial.

Under emperor Augustus, Spain was carved into three provinces, the capital cities were established at what are now Mérida (in Extremadura), Córdoba (Andalucía) and Tarragona (Catalonia). Christianity came to Spain early in the Roman period. The word may have been carried by St Paul himself – he is said to have preached both in Aragón and at Tarragona.

THE VISIGOTHS

Overstretched and increasingly corrupt, Rome watched its far-flung colonies disintegrate, and Germanic tribes, some with a deserved reputation for barbarism, hastened into the vacuum. The Vandals had little to contribute to Spanish culture. However, the Gaulish Visigoths from France did bring a certain constructive influence. Former allies of Rome, they ruled from Toledo, where they displayed their intricate arts and built opulent churches.

The 300-year regime of the Visigoths never achieved any measure of national unity, and eventually foundered on the thorny question of succession. They had introduced to Spain the commendably democratic principle of elective monarchy, but this fostered a web of intrigue and assassination as contenders attempted to secure the crown. These, as well as other problems, were often blamed on the handiest scapegoat: the industrious and successful Jews. They had fared well under the Romans and early Visigoths, but at the start of the 7th century, all non-Christians were forced either to convert to Christianity or face exile.

ENTER THE MOORS

During AD711, an expeditionary force of around 12,000 Berber troops from North Africa sailed across the Straits of Gibraltar

The Alhambra's Patio de los Leones is an exquisite example of Moorish architecture

and poured ashore into Spain. Their expertly planned invasion was led by General Tariq ibn Ziyad (the name Gibraltar is a corruption of Gibel Tariq – Tariq's Rock). His ambition was to spread the influence of Islam.

Within just three years, the Moors had reached the Pyrenees. Their initial success was assisted by ordinary citizens attracted by promises of lower taxes and by serfs offered the chance of freedom. Spanish Jews welcomed the Moors as liberators because, initially at least, the occupation forces stipulated religious tolerance. However, conversion to Islam was later forcefully encouraged, and many Christians chose to embrace the Muslim creed.

The most tangible relics of the Moorish era in Spain are today among the country's greatest tourist attractions: the exquisite palaces, gardens and mosques of Córdoba, Granada and Seville. Thanks to the advanced irrigation techniques imported from North Africa, crops such as rice, cotton and sugar were planted, and lush orchards of almonds, pomegranates, oranges and peaches thrived. Other Moorish innovations made possible the production of paper and glass.

THE CHRISTIANS STRIKE BACK

The Moorish juggernaut that trundled north from Gibraltar in 711 met no serious resistance. It was 11 years before the fragmented defenders of Christian Spain won their first battle. Exiled to the northern territory of Asturias, the Visigothic nobles, led by Pelayo, joined with local mountain folk to strike the first blow in the long-drawn-out Reconquest of Spain. Pelayo's success in 722 at the Battle of Covadonga (the village is now a shrine) sparked off the desire to defeat the Moors and gave heart to a struggle that was to simmer for centuries.

Teruel's Mudéjar-style Torre San Martín

In the middle of the 8th century, the Christians of Asturias, under King Alfonso I, took advantage of a rebellion by Berber troops to occupy neighbouring Galicia. Here, at Santiago de Compostela, the alleged discovery of the tomb of the apostle St James (Santiago) was to make Compostela the religious focus for Spanish Christians and a rallying point for knightly defenders of the Christian faith throughout Europe. More breathing space from Moorish pressure was won in what we now know as Catalonia.

Charlemagne, King of the Franks, captured Catalonia's capital, Barcelona, and established a buffer zone here between Islamic Spain and France. Spanish Christians then seized the advantage and expanded south and west into the area between Catalonia and Asturias, which soon had so many frontier castles that it became known as Castile.

Artistic legacy

The art of medieval Moorish artisans is preserved in today's best Spanish craft buys – ceramics, tooled leather and intricate silverwork.

The Reconquest see-sawed on for hundreds of years, as each side gained and lost territorial advantage under a succession of leaders. Over the centuries, squabbles among the Moors resulted in alliances of convenience with the Christians, and the intermingling of the two cultures was commonplace. Christians who thrived in the Moorish regions were known as Mozarabes, and their Moorish counterparts – Muslim inhabitants of Christian enclaves – were known as Mudéjars. These two names are now attached to the two most important art styles of this period, which are a blend of both Christian and Moorish elements.

Early in the 10th century, the Asturian capital was transferred approximately 120km (75 miles) south from Oviedo to León, a symbolic step deep into former 'infidel' territory. However the Muslims were far from on the run. United under the dictator al-Mansur ('the victorious'), they reclaimed León, Barcelona and Burgos and, in a severe blow to Christian morale, sacked the town of Santiago de Compostela. The death of the charismatic al-Mansur in 1002 revived Christian hopes. In 1010, they succeeded in recapturing al-Mansur's headquarters of Córdoba, and the city of Toledo fell in 1085.

The turning point of the Reconquest is held to be the Battle of Las Navas de Tolosa in 1212. In its wake, the Christian

Bust of El Cid in Plaza de España, Seville

forces regained most of Spain south to Andalucía, to the point where the final Moorish stronghold at Granada was recaptured in 1492.

A SINGULAR NATION

Up until the 15th century, the various regional kingdoms of Spain remained resolutely independent. There were some sporadic moves towards unity, which usually involved strategic marriage contracts, and it was one such royal marriage that united the shrewd Fernando of Aragón and strongly religious and patriotic Isabel of Castile. Under the reign of the Catholic Monarchs, as Pope Alexander VI entitled them, a single Spain was created, comprising most of the nation we know today, though the component parts of the newly united kingdom retained their individuality and their institutions.

Aiming to further unite the country, Fernando and Isabel inaugurated the Inquisition in 1478. Initially intended to safeguard religious orthodoxy under Isabel's influential confessor, the fanatical Tomás de Torquemada, it became a byword for the persecution of Jews, Muslims and, later, Protestants. Several thousand suspected heretics were horribly tortured and many were publicly burned at *autos da fé* (show trials). In 1492, Torquemada convinced Fernando and Isabel to expel the surviving unconverted Jews – perhaps 200,000 in all,

including some of the country's best-educated and most pro-
ductive citizens.

The year 1492 was a momentous one for Spanish history. Not only did it witness the expulsion of the Moors and
the Jews, but also Europe's discovery of the New World by
Genoese explorer Cristobal Colón (Christopher Columbus).
Sponsored by Queen Isabel (who, according to legend,
pawned her own jewels to raise the money), the expedition
and subsequent annexation of the New World territories laid
the foundations for Spain's Golden Age.

THE HABSBURGS

While Fernando and Isabel were Spain personified, their
grandson and heir to the throne, Carlos I, born in Flanders in
1500, could barely compose a sentence in Spanish. Through
his father, Philip, Duke of Burgundy, he inherited extensive

EL CID

The legend of El Cid, Spain's national folk hero, is recounted in the
epic poem *El Cantar de Mío Cid*. Born Rodrigo Díaz de Vivar in around
1040 near Burgos, he was a highly successful soldier of fortune.
Vivar at first fought for the kings of Castile in the battle against the
Moors. When Sancho II died in mysterious circumstances, Vivar hu-
miliated his successor, Alfonso VI, by forcing him to swear publicly
that he had nothing to do with Sancho's death. Exiled for his impu-
dence, Vivar joined the Moors, from whom he received his honorary
title, El Cid (Arabic for 'Lord'). El Cid's greatest victory was in 1094,
when he led a Christian-Moorish army to take Valencia, where he
died in 1099. Encouraged by his death, a Moorish army regrouped
to take the city. El Cid's body was propped on his horse and ridden
before the defending army, which routed the attackers.

possessions in the Low Countries; he was appointed Holy Roman Emperor (Charles V) in 1519. An unpopular king, Carlos alienated his Spanish subjects by appointing Flemish and Burgundian supporters in key posts such as Archbishop of Toledo and regent during his frequent absences. Carlos's expansionist foreign policies consolidated Burgundy and the Netherlands as Spanish provinces. He also annexed Milan and Naples and drew Spain into a series of costly European wars funded from the seemingly bottomless pit of Spain's New World bounty.

In 1556, overwhelmed by his responsibilities, Carlos abdicated in favour of his son, Felipe II. Born and educated in Spain, the new king gave top jobs to Castilians and proclaimed Madrid his capital, thereby converting an unimpressive town of 15,000 into the powerhouse of the greatest empire of the age. As literature and the arts flourished, Felipe worked endlessly to administer his over-extended territories. He captured Portugal, and shared in the glory following the destruction of the Turkish fleet at Lepanto (1571). However, the destruction of the Spanish fleet in the disastrous Armada episode (1588) and the spiralling cost of maintaining the empire eventually robbed Felipe of his health and depleted the Spanish treasury. He died in devout seclusion at El Escorial, the palace-monastery in the hills northwest of Madrid.

Fernando and Isabel greet Christopher Columbus

Although Spain was still the dominant force in Europe at Felipe's death, the Golden Age and empire were on the

Madrid's elegant Retiro Park

wane. Felipe III delegated his responsibilities to his favourites, involved Spain in the Thirty Years' War between the Catholic and the Protestant parts of Europe, and expelled the remaining *Moriscos* (Moorish converts to Christianity after the Reconquest), many of them farmers, thereby precipitating an agricultural crisis.

The final century of the Habsburg era saw a gradual, then a rapid decline in Spanish fortunes. Ironically, in contrast to the severe loss of territorial possessions and despite the ravages of war, pestilence and famine, the works of Velázquez, Zurbarán, Murillo and Ribera bear witness to the achievements of Spanish artists of the age.

The last of the Spanish Habsburgs, Carlos II, died heirless in 1700. His crown went to the Duke of Anjou, grandson of Louis XIV of France, who claimed the title as Felipe V of Spain. Archduke Charles of Austria (another Habsburg) contested the claim, which sparked the War of the Spanish Succession, ended by the Treaty of Utrecht in 1713.

BOURBONS ON THE THRONE

Felipe V eventually secured the throne, but his diminishing empire was now shorn of Belgium, Luxembourg, Milan, Sicily and Sardinia. To add insult to injury, Britain snatched strategic Gibraltar. The most successful Spanish king of the 18th century, Carlos III, recruited capable administrators, disbanded the Inquisition, invigorated the economy and paved the streets of Madrid. But Spain came increasingly under the power of France during the Bourbon period.

After the defeat of the Franco-Spanish fleet by the British at the Battle of Trafalgar in 1805, Carlos IV had to abdicate. Napoleon tried to appoint his brother Joseph as José I, but the Spanish rose against the French, resulting in the Peninsular War (known in Spain as the War of Independence). In 1814, with the help of British troops led by the Duke of Wellington, the French were finally ousted. While all this was going on, a number of Spain's most profitable American colonies took advantage of her preoccupation to secure their independence.

Italian planes bomb the Republicans in the Civil War

With Fernando VII on the throne, a Bourbon king once again ruled Spain, but the country miserably failed to prosper. Political infighting, a repressive monarchy and anti-clerical revolts led to the domestic Carlist Wars. The 19th century ended with another disaster as Cuba, Puerto Rico and the Philippines were lost in the Spanish-American War.

THE SPANISH CIVIL WAR

Spain escaped the horrors of World War I, watching the carnage from a position of neutrality. Alfonso XIII backed the dictatorship of General Miguel Primo de Rivera (1923–30), but went into exile (never to return) after anti-royalist forces won a landslide victory in the 1931 elections. The new Republic was riven with bitter ideological conflicts, between the Left and Right. A left-wing victory in the 1936 elections and the assassination of the Monarchist leader, Calvo Sotelo, ignited nationalist and conservative fears of a Marxist revolution. Monarchists, clergy and the right-wing Falange organisation united behind the Movimiento Nacional, led by General Francisco Franco. Meanwhile, a coalition of liberals, communists, socialists and anarchists cast their lot with the newly elected Spanish government.

The outcome was the Civil War: three years of horrific bloodshed and destruction which gutted towns and cities and claimed between 50,000 and 75,000 lives, as father fought son and region battled against region. Franco emerged victorious, but the country was shattered, both physically and emotionally.

THE NEW SPAIN

Franco ruled the country for almost 40 years, a period of political repression accompanied from the 1960s onwards by economic development. On Franco's death in 1975 his chosen successor, Juan Carlos de Borbón, grandson of Alfonso XIII, was crowned king. He oversaw an extraordinarily swift and smooth transition from dictatorship to democracy. A new constitution was approved that devolved many powers to 17 newly created 'autonomous' regions.

The Socialist party held power for much of the 1980s and 1990s. During this time Spain rejoined the mainstream of international life, becoming a member of Nato and the EU. In the momentous year of 1992 a World Fair was held in Seville and the Olympic Games in Barcelona. A right-of-centre government succeeded the Socialists but was ousted from power in 2004 following the traumatic terrorist bombing of Madrid commuter trains. In 2007 Spain was hit by the credit crisis, which badly affected its important construction industry, and forced a rethink of economic priorities.

The year 2011 saw a return to power of the centre right Popular Party (PP) led by PM Mariano Rajoy. Rajoy managed to lift the economy but his popularity plummeted following a series of notorious political and economic scandals that also affected King Juan Carlos I and his family. As a result, the ageing monarch abdicated in favour of his son who became King Felipe VI in 2014. Recent years have also been marked by the increasing popularity of new parties including the left-wing Podemos and the centrist Ciudadanos. Allied with other grassroots movements across the country, they scored their first major success in the regional and autonomous elections of 2015, taking control of Spain's largest cities including Madrid and Barcelona.

King Felipe VI is the new king of Spain

HISTORICAL LANDMARKS

*c.*3000BC Bronze-Age Celts in the north, Iberians in the south.
1100BC Phoenicians found Gadir (Cádiz).
3rd century BC Carthaginians conquer much of Spain.
1st century BC Romans complete their conquest of Spain.
1st century AD Christianity introduced.
6th century Visigoths make Toledo their capital.
711 Moors take Andalucía and control most of Spain.
722 Christian Reconquest begins at Covadonga.
758 Córdoba becomes the Moorish capital.
1469 Fernando and Isabel's marriage kickstarts Spain's unification.
1478 Inauguration of the Inquisition.
1492 Fall of Granada to the Christians completes the Reconquest.
Jewish and Arab expulsion. Columbus' voyage.
1516 Carlos I inherits the Spanish throne.
1556–98 Felipe II rules from Madrid.
1588 Defeat of the Spanish Armada.
1618–48 The Thirty Years' War.
1701–14 War of Spanish Succession. Felipe V wins crown.
1804–14 War of Independence (Spanish Peninsular War).
1898 The Spanish-American War: end of empire.
1914–18 Spain is neutral in World War I.
1923–30 Primo de Rivera's dictatorship supported by King Alfonso XIII.
1936 Left-wing government elected; start of Civil War.
1939 Republicans defeated; Franco in power.
1975 Franco dies; King Juan Carlos accedes.
1978 New democratic constitution ratified.
1986 Spain joins the EU.
2004 Ten bombs kill 201 on Madrid commuter trains. Socialists elected.
2010 Spain wins the football World Cup in South Africa.
2014 King Juan Carlos I abdicates in favour of his son Felipe.
2015 Regional and autonomous elections: new parties including Podemos and Ciudadanos make important gains securing control over Madrid and Barcelona ahead of general elections in November.

WHERE TO GO

MADRID

Settled by the Romans in the 2nd century BC, **Madrid ❶** was occupied by the Moors in AD711. Under Mohammed I, the Moors fortified the town in 865, and made it a walled city. Just over two centuries later, in 1083, Madrid was reconquered by King Alfonso VI. Fernando IV summoned the Courts of the Kingdom in 1309, the Catholic Monarchs ordered the de-fortification of the city's walls and gates in 1476 and, in 1561, Felipe II moved the court here from Toledo, making Madrid the capital of a vast empire.

The early part of the next century, during the Habsburg era, saw the addition of the Plaza Mayor. The House of Bourbon succeeded the Habsburgs, and it was this dynasty that was responsible for many of the grand buildings and monuments that adorn the city today. Among these are the Royal Palace, completed in 1764; the Alcalá gate, raised in 1778 to honour Carlos III's entry into the city as king, and the Prado Museum constructed between 1785 and 1819. During the Spanish Civil War, the city was subject to a siege by the Nationalist forces, whose eventual entry into Madrid effectively ended hostilities.

Madrid is the largest city in Spain and, at an elevation of 655m (2,100ft), the highest capital in Europe. The ambiance of this bustling modern city reflects an intriguing blend of old and new. It also makes a good base for exploring several nearby historic cities. The best way to get around town is by the efficient *metro* (underground) system.

The best place to start is the busy **Plaza Puerta del Sol** (Gate of the Sun), the hub of 10 converging streets. This is literally the crossroads of Spain, known as 'Kilometre 0' in the country's highway system, and home to an imposing

Guards at the Royal Palace, Madrid

equestrian statue of Carlos III and a smaller statue depicting Madrid's coat-of-arms – a bear standing against a *madroño* (arbutus, or strawberry) tree.

PLAZA MAYOR

A few blocks west is the **Plaza Mayor** (Main Square), a 17th-century architectural masterpiece. Its broad arcades surround a vast, traffic-free, cobbled rectangle, once used as the inner-city showground for bullfights, pageants and even public executions. Today, an equestrian statue of Felipe III surveys rows of outdoor cafés and lively summer-season festivals. The plaza's most famous houses are the **Casa de la Panadería** (Bakers' Guild), which holds the Plaza Mayor Tourist Information Centre, and the **Casa de la Carnicería** (Butchers' Guild), whose facades are decorated with a series of vibrant, and even mildly erotic, paintings.

Plaza Mayor at night

Continuing west on Calle Mayor, **Plaza de la Villa** juxtaposes stately 16th- and 17th-century buildings of differing styles. These include the lovely **Casa de Cisneros**, which belongs to the ornate and delicate style of architecture known as Plateresque (*platero* means silversmith), and the towering Habsburg-era **Ayuntamiento** (City Hall).

The bright lights of Gran Vía

PALACIO REAL

To the north is the **Palacio Real** **B** (Royal Palace; Apr–Sept daily 10am–8pm, Oct–Mar daily 10am–6pm; closed on state occasions; www.patrimonionacional.es), set among formal gardens on a bluff overlooking the Manzanares Valley. Felipe V commissioned this imposing French-style palace on the site of the old Moorish fort, and furnished its 2,000 rooms (only the Hermitage in St Petersburg has more) in a suitably regal fashion. It was the principal residence of Spanish kings from Felipe's time in the mid-18th century until Alfonso XIII was exiled in 1931. Visit at your leisure, or join one of the hour-long tours that take in around 50 rooms, including the over-whelmingly rococo Gasparini Room, the Ceremonial Dining Room with seating for 145 guests, and the Throne Room with its stunning Tiepolo ceiling frescoes. Also worth seeing are the Royal Armoury, the Pharmacy and the Library.

The **Gran Vía** **C** is Madrid's main thoroughfare. Lined with shops, hotels, restaurants, theatres, cafés and night-clubs, it cuts a wide path west to east from Plaza de España

Roy Lichtenstein's Woman in Bath at the Museo Thyssen-Bornemisza

to the busy round **Plaza de la Cibeles**, so named for the Cybele Fountain that is adorned with a sculpture of a Greek fertility goddess.

ART COLLECTIONS

Art lovers are spoilt for choice in Madrid. One of the city's fascinating hidden treasures is the **Monasterio de las Descalzas Reales** (Tue–Sat 10am–2pm and 4–6.30pm, Sun 10am–3pm; guided tours; www.patrimonio nacional.es), located behind the El Corte Ingles store at the Puerta del Sol. Once a retreat for the Kings of Castile, this 16th-century convent has been handsomely endowed with a wealth of art treasures. The **Real Academía de Bellas Artes de San Fernando**, also close to the Puerta del Sol, has a fine collection of paintings by Goya (Tue–Sun 10am–3pm; closed Aug; free on Wed except holidays; www.realacademiabellasartessanfernando.com).

Housed in 18th-century neoclassical grandeur, the **Museo del Prado D** (Mon–Sat 10am–8pm, Sun until 7pm; free daily last two hours; www.museodelprado.es), has fabulous art treasures amassed by the Spanish monarchy. The Prado houses the world's greatest collection of Spanish paintings, and a particularly strong set of Italian and Flemish masterpieces. If time is short, plan ahead and decide what you most want to see. Likely top-of-the-list sights are works by

El Greco (1541–1614), Ribera (1591–1652), Zurbarán (1598–1664), Felipe IV's court painter Velázquez (1599–1660, whose *Las Meninas*, or *Maids of Honour*, is said to be Spain's favourite painting), Murillo (1617–82), and magnificent Goya (1746–1828). Of the Dutch and Flemish masters, be sure not to miss works by Hieronymus Bosch (known as 'El Bosco') and Rubens. The Italian Old Masters include works by Raphael, Titian and Tintoretto.

Across the Plaza Cánovas del Castillo, the **Museo Thyssen-Bornemisza** (Mon noon–4pm, Tue–Sun 10am–7pm; free Mon; www.museothyssen.org) spans 700 years of artistic endeavour from the Italian primitives to Pop Art. Just a short distance to the south the **Museo Nacional Centro de Arte Reina Sofía** (Mon and Wed–Sat 10am–9pm, Sun 10am–2.30pm; charge, free last two hours; www.museoreinasofia.es) has important collections of modern art and many masterpieces by Picasso – including his monumental mural, *Guernica*, inspired by the Civil War bombing of a Basque village.

The impressive **Museo Arqueológico Nacional** (Tue–Sat 9.30am–8pm, Sun 9.30am–3pm; free Sat after 2.30pm and Sun am, www.man.es) contains the celebrated Celtiberian bust known as *La Dama de Elche* and a wealth of Visigothic treasures discovered at Toledo. In the gardens is a replica of the prehistoric Altamira caves (see page 86), complete with wall paintings.

If the sightseeing and the bustle get too much, the enormous **Parque del Retiro**

The big three

Art lovers intent on seeing Madrid's Big Three art museums – the Prado, Thyssen-Bornemisza, and the Reina Sofía – would do well to acquire the Paseo del Arte voucher. This allows visits to all three museums for a single price (around €25), a considerable saving on the individual admission prices. It's valid for a year.

behind the Prado is a favourite spot for Madrileños out for a stroll. Originally a 17th-century Habsburg hunting ground, it offers 121 hectares (300 acres) of leafy avenues, flower beds and park benches, as well as a rose garden, boating lake and Sunday morning sideshows. There are also cafés, exhibitions in the Palacio de Cristal and Palacio de Velázquez (free; www.museoreinasofia.es) and a botanical garden founded by Carlos III in 1781.

AROUND MADRID

ARANJUEZ

One of the most popular day-trips from Madrid is to the royal town of **Aranjuez** ❷, 48km (30 miles) south by train or motorway. The best way to get here in summer is from Atocha station on board the Tren de la Fresa (www.renfe.com), a steam train running along Spain's second-oldest railway line built in 1849. The main reason to make the journey is to stroll in the pleasant formal gardens, laid out for the leisure of the court, which nudge up to the banks of the Río Tajo (River Tagus). It is not hard to see how they could have been the inspiration for Spain's most famous piece of music, Joaquín Rodrigo's *Concierto de Aranjuez*.

Not to be missed is the **Palacio Real** (Tue–Sun 10am–6pm, summer until 8pm; www.patrimonionacional.es), a royal palace which stands at the heart of Aranjuez. It took shape over 200 years, evolving through the reigns of eight monarchs, but in its present form it is mostly the work of 18th-century baroque inspiration. The guided tour leads visitors through a succession of ornate rooms including the throne room, king's smoking room and porcelain room. From outside the palace two bridges lead over a narrow branch of the river to the **Jardín de la Isla** (Island Garden; free), which combines Spanish, Flemish and Moorish influences in its classical fountains and clipped hedges.

Toledo is almost surrounded by the River Tagus

TOLEDO

Located on a strategic hill protected by the encircling River Tagus, **Toledo** ❸ is a fascinating historical city and a Unesco World Heritage Site. Conquered by the Romans in 193BC, Toledo became the political and religious capital of the Visigoths in the 5th century AD after they had overrun the Vandals. After the Moors invaded Spain, in AD711, the city was incorporated into the Córdoba Emirate. When the Emirate disintegrated in 1012, it became the capital of an independent kingdom. In 1085 Alfonso VI of León reconquered Toledo and made it his capital, a status it retained until 1561 when Felipe II moved the capital to Madrid. This marked the beginning of the decline of the importance of Toledo, even though it has remained the seat of the Primate of Spain.

Unquestionably the most important monument in the city is the massive **cathedral** (Mon–Sat 10am–6pm, Sun 2–6pm; free Sun pm; www.catedralprimada.es). The first one on this site was built jointly by the Visigoth King Recaredo I and the

The stunning reredos inside Toledo's cathedral

first Bishop of Toledo, San Eugenio. Converted into a mosque by the Moors, it was not until 1227 that King Fernando III, 'the Saint', began construction of the present building. It was not completed until the 16th century and as it incorporates numerous architectural styles it is known as the 'Museum Cathedral'. The **coro**, or choir, and main altar reredos are marvels of woodcarving. Just behind the main chapel, Narciso Tomé's baroque **Transparente** is an 18th-century masterpiece, and in the **Sala Capitular** (Chapter House) there is an intricate ceiling in the Mudéjar style. If you look up you'll see hats hanging precariously from the vaulting. They are suspended over plaques that indicate tombs of Primates buried below; each hat belonging to the respective Primate.

Don't miss, either, the **Tesoro** (Treasury) with religious artworks, including 18 paintings by El Greco, and Enrique de Arfe's Monstrance. Made of solid silver and gold, it has more than 5,600 parts and weighs a substantial 200kg (430lb).

Dominating the city is the enormous **Alcázar** (Thu–Tue 10am–5pm; free Sun; www.ejercito.mde.es), a fortress destroyed and rebuilt many times since the Roman era. The fortress houses an **Army Museum** with displays relating to the dramatic 72-day siege.

EL GRECO IN TOLEDO

The painter El Greco is inextricably linked with Toledo. His first commission was to paint the reredos at the Cistercian convent of **Santo Domingo el Antiguo** which, founded in 1085 by King Alfonso VI, is the oldest monastery in Toledo (11am–1.30pm and 4–7pm, closed Sun am). More famously, his *Burial of the Count of Orgaz*, a fascinating depiction of local noblemen attending the count's funeral, is on display at the church of **Santo Tomé** (daily 10am–6.45pm, winter until 5.45pm; www.santotome.org) – also notable for its landmark Mudéjar tower. The young boy attending upon the saints is considered to be a likeness of El Greco's son, and on a handkerchief dangling from the boy's pocket he signed his name, Doménico Theotokopouli, and the date, 1583. More of El Greco's work, including a *Crucifixion* with Toledo as the backdrop, can be found at the 16th-century **Museo-Hospital de Santa Cruz** (Mon–Sat 10am–7pm, Sun 10am–2.30pm; free last hour).

Just downhill from Santo Tomé is a restored 14th-century building El Greco lived in for a number of years. It now forms the **Casa-Museo de El Greco** (Tue–Sat 9.30am–7.30pm, winter until 6pm, Sun 10am–3pm; free Sat pm and Sun; http://museo delgreco.mcu.es), refurbished for the 400th anniversary of El Greco's death in 2014, and brings together some of El Greco's work, as well as pieces by Murillo.

TOLEDO STEEL

Toledo is famous all over the world for the quality of its steel, and swords have been forged here since Roman times. According to legend, the special property of the steel is inherited from the magical water of the River Tagus (Río Tajo). Look for damascene steel souvenirs. This is a craft unique to the city, which involves inlaying black steel with decorative gold, copper and silver filigree.

Nearby is **La Sinagoga del Tránsito** built by Samuel Levi, a 14th-century financier and a friend of King Pedro I of Castile. Muslim artists adorned the walls with intricate filigree and Hebrew inscriptions from the Psalms. The synagogue houses the **Museo Sefardí** (Sephardic Museum; Mar–Oct Tue–Sat 9.30am–7.30pm, Sun 10am–3pm, Nov–Feb Tue–Sat 9.30am–6pm, Sun 10am–3pm; http://museosefardi.mcu. es). Not far away is the **Santa Maria la Blanca** synagogue, which resembles a mosque and has a simplicity of style that enhances its ambiance.

Just down the street is a fine church with royal connections. Fernando and Isabel, whose emblems of the different realms combined by their marriage lie either side of the altar, built **San Juan de los Reyes** (St John of the Kings; www.sanjuande losreyes.org) to celebrate victory at the Battle of Toro in 1476. In a mix of Mudéjar, Gothic and Renaissance styles, it was also meant to be the Catholic Monarchs' final resting place. That was before they became enchanted with Granada, the Moors' last stronghold, which was captured in 1492. There is also a superb double-height cloister with elaborate stone carvings.

Another must-see is the 10th-century **El Cristo de la Luz** (Christ of the Light), a mosque until the Reconquest and the only building in the city from that era to have survived in its original condition.

ÁVILA

Situated 112km (70 miles) northwest of Madrid, at an altitude of 1,128m (3,700ft) above sea level, **Ávila** ❹ is the highest city in Spain. With origins in the Celtiberian era, it was Christianised in the 1st century AD, and after nearly three centuries of Moorish rule was reconquered by King Alfonso VI in 1085. After the Reconquest the city was repopulated by Christian knights, who began work on what is unquestionably Ávila's most dominant feature: **Las Murallas** – the walls. These are, on average, over 3.6m (12ft) high and 2.7m (9ft) thick. Built into their nearly 2.7km (1.6-mile) length are nine gateways and 90 towers. Noblemen were responsible for defending a particular section of the wall. Consequently, many elegantly fortified mansions were built near, or as an integral part of, the walls. Even the 12th- to 16th-century **cathedral**, (http://catedralavila. vocces.com); combining Romanesque, Gothic and Renaissance elements, has a *cimorro* (fortified head) built into the walls.

Ávila's spiritual influence is a legacy of St Teresa, who was beatified on 12 March, 1622. She was born here in 1515 and her influence, in the shape of churches, convents and statues, can be seen throughout the city. A Catholic visionary and advocate of Carmelite thought, she founded no fewer than 17 convents throughout Spain and wrote prolifically. She lived for 30 years in the **Convento de la Encarnación**, outside the city walls, first as a novice and for the last three years as prioress.

Ávila cathedral statuary

Just outside the city walls, the **Basílica de San Vicente** – commemorating St Vincent of Zaragoza and his two sisters, who were martyred in the 4th century – is noted for an extraordinary tomb topped by a bizarre oriental canopy.

Although some distance away from the town centre,

the **Monasterio de Santo Tomás** belonging to the Dominican Order should not be missed. Dating from 1482, it was used frequently by the Catholic Monarchs as a summer residence. Fernando and Isabel's only son, Don Juan, died here at the age of 19 and his impressive sepulchre is in the chapel. Treasures acquired by missionaries on their Far Eastern travels are exhibited here in the Oriental Art Museum (www. monasteriosantotomas.com).

After viewing Ávila up close, drive or take a bus across the Río Adaja to the monument called **Los Cuatro Postes** (The Four Posts). Curious in itself, it consists of four Doric columns connected by cornices, each of which is decorated with the city's coats-of-arms, with a stone cross in the centre. More importantly, the hill offers a panoramic view of the whole of medieval Ávila, which is especially impressive when floodlit at night.

SAN LORENZO DE EL ESCORIAL

At an elevation of 1,065m (3,494ft) in the foothills of the Sierra de Guadarrama, by the town of El Escorial, 49km (30 miles) northwest of Madrid, you will find a building of absolutely massive proportions. Visible from miles away, the monastery of **San Lorenzo de El Escorial ⑤** (Tue–Sun 10am–8pm, Oct–Mar until 6pm; free last three hours Wed–Thu; www. patrimonionacional.es) was commissioned in 1557 by Felipe II to commemorate his victory over Henri II of France at the Battle of San Quentín, an event that took place on 10 August, the Feast Day of San Lorenzo (St Lawrence). Extended over the years, it has 86 stairways, more than 1,200 doors and 2,600 windows, summing up the physical and spiritual superlatives of the empire's Golden Age.

The monastery is actually a multifaceted complex, comprising royal living quarters, a basilica, monastery, pantheon, elaborate library, and art galleries and museum all under one roof. The **apartments of Felipe II** are modest in comfort but rich in art, and include a fantastic triptych by Hieronymus Bosch. The **Palacio Real** (Royal Palace) has a succession of lavishly decorated rooms, notably the Sala de las Batallas, adorned with frescoes depicting complex battle scenes, and fine tapestries. Of the dozens of works of art collected in the great **basilica** – which is part Sotocoro (people's church), part monastic church and part royal – none attracts more admiration than Cellini's life-sized marble crucifix. Felipe II died at the palace in 1598 and, along with the remains of almost all Spain's monarchs and their families from the 17th century onwards, is buried in the elaborate royal **pantheon**. The **library**, with its baroque ceiling adorned with a series of magnificent frescoes by Tibaldi, is particularly spectacular and contains some 40,000 rare books, plus priceless and beautiful manuscripts. The **New Museums** display masterpieces by

San Lorenzo de El Escorial, where Felipe II lived and died

Ribera, Tintoretto, Velázquez and El Greco. In 1984 El Escorial was declared a World Heritage Monument by Unesco.

VALLE DE LOS CAÍDOS

Just around the mountain is another monument of enormous proportions, albeit one of a very different type. After the Spanish Civil War, Franco wanted to build a monument to commemorate those who died during the hostilities. For the site he chose the V-shaped valley called Cuelgamuros, in the Sierra de Guadarrama, known today as the **Valle de los Caídos** ❻ (Valley of the Fallen). The tone of the monument is distinctly Nationalist, and as a surviving legacy of Franco's rule it remains controversial. Of the two disparate parts, the most visible is a huge cross standing 150m (492ft) high and 46m (150ft) wide, set upon the summit of a small mountain. On weekends and holidays a funicular takes visitors to the base of the cross where they may investigate the plinth adorned by four enormous figures.

Equally grand is the underground **Basilica** (Tue–Sun 10am–7pm, Oct–Mar until 6pm; www.valledeloscaidos.es). Carved 240m (786ft) deep into the granite mountain, it is reached via a tunnel and opens out into a gigantic dome that is almost directly under the cross outside. The tombstones of Franco and José Antonio Primo de Rivera, founder of the Falangist Party, occupy a privileged position. A series of Flemish tapestries dating from 1553 decorates the church, and ossuaries in the crypt (closed to the public) contain the remains of tens of thousands of the dead, of both sides, from the Civil War.

SEGOVIA

Segovia ❼, 88km (55 miles) northwest of Madrid, is an unspoiled medieval town that strategically sits on a high promontory between two rivers. High on the rocks overlooking

Segovia's Alcázar

the confluence of the rivers is the **Alcázar** (daily summer 10am–7pm, winter 10am–6pm; www.alcazardesegovia.com), Segovia's fairytale royal castle. Although originally constructed in the 12th and 13th centuries, much of it dates from the following two centuries. It became a royal favourite – Isabel left from here to be proclaimed queen – but was converted to a Royal Artillery School in the late 18th century and was largely rebuilt after a fire in 1862. Today, it houses a museum of weaponry, and you can climb the 152 steps to the top of the tower for spectacular views.

The towering **cathedral** was begun in 1525, after the original one – on a different site – was destroyed during the Comuneros War. As a consequence, it is the last of the great Spanish cathedrals to be built in the Gothic style. Fine stained-glass windows illuminate the interior.

Segovia is best known, however, for the **Roman aqueduct**, both a work of art and a triumph of engineering. Dating from the 1st or 2nd century AD, it has 165 arches covering a length of 728m (2,392ft) and it reaches 28m (92ft) in height. Amazingly, the granite stones are held together by nothing but their own weight.

Segovia has an array of other interesting churches, monasteries and museums, the best of which is a small church near the Alcázar. The **Vera Cruz** church dates from the 13th century and was probably founded by the Knights Templar. Its 12-sided design is believed to have been copied from the Church of the Holy Sepulchre in Jerusalem. It is unique in Spain but similar to many other churches that the knights founded in Portugal. Outside Segovia is the royal summer palace of **La Granja de San Ildefonso**, with its magnificent formal gardens.

BARCELONA

Of Phoenician origins, **Barcelona** ❽ flourished under the Romans, and remains of the walls constructed during that era are still visible in the city's so-called Gothic Quarter; foundations of the Roman town have been excavated from beneath the City History Museum. The period of Visigothic rule saw a decline in importance and although the Moors swept across the Iberian peninsula in the early 8th century they were unable to control this area for long. In 801, following its recapture by the Franks, the city was incorporated into Charlemagne's empire as the capital of the county of Barcelona, the most dominant of the Catalan counties. For nearly five centuries, unlike in other parts of the country, Barcelona and Catalunya remained Christian, giving this region an entirely different character from the rest of Spain. Subsequently, it was united with the neighbouring kingdom of Aragón in the 12th century, thus ensuing a period of flourishing maritime trade.

The unification of Spain under Fernando of Aragón and Isabel of Castile in 1469 led to attempts to suppress the well-established institutions of this dynamic and strongly independent region. For centuries, Barcelona repeatedly struggled to maintain its unique identity. During the Spanish Civil War it served as the capital of the Republican forces and was almost the last city to fall to Franco. As a result, Barcelona was singled out for harsh reprisals, and the Catalan language was suppressed. Now, with a well-earned reputation for its style and architecture, particularly that of Antoni Gaudí, Barcelona is the thriving capital of a largely

Palau Güell rooftop spire

autonomous region where the people display a passion for all things Catalan, including their language; in fact half of them would rather see Catalonia as an independent country.

LA RAMBLA

Without doubt, **La Rambla** Ⓐ, linking the busy **Plaça de Catalunya** with the harbour, is Barcelona's most popular street. Everyone comes to walk along its wide tree-lined promenade, with its market stalls and brightly coloured flower kiosks, its open-air restaurants and bars, as well as street artists performing impromptu shows and living statues posing for photographs. Along its route are numerous places of interest, including the ever-popular **La Boqueria** (www.boqueria.info) – the 19th-century covered market

Strolling along La Rambla

that is a city highlight – and the famous **Liceu** opera house (expanded and completely refurbished after a devastating fire in 1998). A little further, the **Museu d'Art Contemporani de Barcelona MACBA** (Mon, Wed, Fri 11am–8pm, Thu until 9pm, Sat 10am–8pm, Sun 10am–3pm; www.macba.cat), a contemporary art collection housed in a modern white building by Richard Meier, has become a symbol of the transformation of the medieval Raval district into an artistic and vibrant neighbourhood. The adjacent **Centro de Cultura Contemporánea de Barcelona** (CCCB; www.cccb.org) is a modern art centre housed in an 19th-century almshouse.

Further south, Gaudí's fortress-like **Palau Güell** (http://palauguell.cat) on Nou de la Rambla, was built for his major sponsor in 1885. Across La Rambla a passage leads into the café-filled arcades of **Plaça Reial**, adorned by a central fountain and iron lanterns, both designed by Gaudí, and 35 palm trees. Towards the bottom of the Rambla is the **Museu Marítim** (daily 10am–8pm; free Sun from 3pm; www.mmb.

cat), which traces 700 years of Barcelona's maritime history and is well worth a visit just for the architecture of the enormous ship-building sheds. At the bottom of the Rambla, the **Monument a Colóm** – honouring Christopher Columbus (Cristóbal Colóm) – towers over the harbour area.

The harbour area at the end of La Rambla has been transformed in recent years. Traditional *golondrinas* boats offer a fun way of seeing the harbour, or you can cross **Port Vell** to the Moll d'Espanya by a wooden promenade. There you'll find a modern complex consisting of shops, restaurants, an IMAX theatre and the **Aquàrium de Barcelona** (July–Aug daily 9.30am–11pm, June and Sept 9.30am–9.30pm, rest of year

GETTING AROUND BARCELONA

Barcelona's many attractions are widely separated from each other. It helps that there is an excellent public transport system, and the buses and metro (underground) will take you almost everywhere. A neat option is the Bus Turistic, which has two main routes – the red northern route and blue southern route (with four transfer points). Both depart from the Plaça de Catalunya from 9am daily. An extra green route operates in summer. Each route provides a hop-on, hop-off service around all the main sights. Tickets – available on board, at tourist offices or at https://barcelonasmartmoving.com – include discounted admission to many museums and attractions, including the cable car, funicular and tram rides for Montjuïc and Tibidabo. Also worth considering is the Barcelona Card, which can be purchased for periods of three to five days and offers free public transport as well as more than 100 discounts at museums, places of entertainment, shops, restaurants and even the Aerobus (airport bus). There is also the option of just buying a travelcard (Hola BCN), valid for two to five days on all public transport (www.tmb.cat).

Mon–Fri 9.30am–9pm, Sat–Sun until 9.30pm; www.aquarium bcn.com) – one of Europe's largest.

BARRI GÒTIC

The narrow alleyways and historic buildings of **Barri Gòtic** Ⓑ cluster around the imposing **Catedral** (Mon–Fri 8am–7.30pm, Sat–Sun 8am–8pm, cloisters 8.30am–7pm, charge between 1–5pm; www.catedralbcn.org). The third to exist on this site, it dates from the 13th century but has a 19th-century facade. There is also a graceful garden cloister. In the square outside you will see performances of the Catalan national dance on summer weekends. There are two very interesting museums nearby: the **Museu d'Història de la Ciutat** (City History Museum; Tue–Sat 10am–7pm, Sun 10am–8pm; http://museuhistoria.bcn.cat) leads through the underground Roman foundations to the **Palau Reial Major**, the former Royal Palace; the **Museu Frederic Marès** (Tue–Sat 10am–7pm, Sun 10am–8pm; free Sun from 3pm; www.museumares.bcn.cat), founded by a collector named Marès, contains an eclectic miscellany of religious objects and art from around the world with pieces dating from the Middle Ages.

Among the galleries on Carrer de Montcada in the neighbouring district of El Born, the **Museu Picasso** Ⓒ (Tue–Sun 10am–7pm, Thu until 9.30pm; free Sun from 3pm; www.museu picasso.bcn.cat) is the city's most popular museum. Entrance is through the 15th-century Palau Aguilar, and the collection includes many of Picasso's early works, major pieces from his Blue and Pink periods, the idiosyncratic *Las Meninas* series (based on the Velázquez masterpiece in Madrid's Prado art gallery), as well as ceramics. Across the street is the new **Museu Europeu d'Art Modern MEAM** (Tue–Sun 10am–8pm; www.meam.es), specialising in 20th- and 21st-century figurative art. Still on Carrer de Montcada be sure, also, to pop into the **El Xampanyet** bar at No. 22 where, besides delicious *tapas*, a refreshingly light, sparkling, champagne-like *cava* is served.

The pure, Gothic beauty of the 14th-century **Santa María del Mar** church (Mon–Sat 9am–1pm, 5–8.30pm, Sun 10am–2pm, 5–8pm; www. santamariadelmarbarcelona. org) can be seen at the bottom of Montcada.

PARC DE LA CIUTADELLA

To the east, the green expanse of the **Parc de la Ciutadella**, its name derived from an 18th-century prison torn

Parc de la Ciutadella fountain

down with much glee in 1869, encompasses paths, gardens and ponds, and an elaborate Gaudí fountain. It also has the Catalan parliament and the **Parc Zoològic** (www.zoobarcelona.cat), one of Europe's better zoos.

MONTJUÏC

Barcelona's historic Jewish community once lived on the slopes of Montjuïc (Hill of the Jews), which looms up behind the harbour, crowned by the 17th-century **Castillo de Montjuïc** (daily 10am–6pm; summer until 8pm; free Sun from 3pm) and reached by cable car, funicular or bus. The castle offers spectacular views of the city. Down below is the **Font Mágica** (magic fountain), which is illuminated on summer evenings. Nearby is the art centre **CaixaForum Barcelona** (daily

10am–8pm, summer Wed until 11pm; www.fundacio.lacaixa.es), located in a converted *modernista* factory design by Josep Puig i Cadafalch. Other attractions of the area include the **Fundació Joan Miró** (Tue–Wed, Fri–Sat 10am–7pm, July–Sept until 8pm, Thu 10am–9pm, Sun and holidays 10am–2.30pm; www.fmirobcn.org), and facilities left from the 1992 Olympic Games including the main stadium, swimming pools and the **Torre de Calatrava,** one of the symbols of those games. There is also the **Poble Espanyol** (Spanish Village; daily from 9am, Mon to 8pm, Tue–Thu and Sun to midnight, Fri to 3am, Sat to 4am; www.poble-espanyol.com) which showcases Spanish architecture and traditions with miniature replicas of palaces, castles and churches, plus artisans' workshops, concerts and evening flamenco performances. World-class collections of Romanesque and Gothic art are displayed in the **Museu Nacional d'Art de Catalunya** (winter Tue–Sat 10am–6pm, Sun 10am–3pm, summer Tue–Sat 10am–8pm, Sun 10am–3pm; free Sat from 3pm; www.museunacional.cat) in the imposing Palacio Nacional, which also contains the **Museu d'Art**

MODERNISME

Modernisme, a movement related to the design styles in vogue in Europe in the late 19th century – French art nouveau, German and Austrian Jugendstil – was a rebellion against the rigid forms and colourless stone and plaster of classical architecture. In Barcelona the new style assumed nationalist motifs and significance, which may be why it has been so carefully preserved here. Although there was an entire school of *modernista* architects working in Barcelona from the late 19th century until the 1930s, it is customary to speak of the 'Big Three': Antoni Gaudí, who left such a personal mark on the city, Lluís Domènech i Montaner and Josep Puig i Cadafalch.

Modern, with its notable collection of 19th- and 20th-century Catalan works, as well as *modernista* furniture.

GAUDÍ'S LEGACY

Of course, Barcelona is also famous for Antoni Gaudí's unique and eccentric archi-tectural designs. The largest of these is the surrealistic

Inside the Sagrada Família

Sagrada Família (Holy Family) church (daily 9am–6pm, summer until 8pm; www.sagradafamilia.org). An unfinished masterpiece started in 1882 (and still in progress), its 100m (330ft) towers are local landmarks. Other Gaudían highlights include tours of the **Casa Milà–La Pedrera** rooftops and one of the apartments at Passeig de Gràcia 92 (Mon–Fri 9am–10pm, Sat–Sun 10am–2pm, 6–10pm; www.lapedrera.com), the **Casa Batlló** (daily 9am–9pm; www.casabatllo.es) down the street at No. 43, and the fascinating **Park Güell**, (8am–9.30pm, Mar–May and Sep–Oct until 8pm, winter until 6pm; www.parkguell.cat) with its colourful tile mosaics.

PEDRALBES

On the western edge of the city, the beautiful **Monestir Santa María de Pedralbes** (Apr–Sept Tue–Fri 10am–5pm, Sat until 7pm and Sun until 8pm, Oct–Mar Tue–Fri 10am–2pm, Sat–Sun 10am–5pm; free Sun from 3pm; http://monestir pedralbes.bcn.cat) deserves a special mention. Founded by Queen Elisenda in 1326, it has a charming cloister and an exceptional selection of paintings on loan from the Thyssen-Bornemisza art collection in Madrid. In the western hills

Montserrat monastery

overlooking Barcelona, the popular amusement park at **Tibidabo** (www.tibidabo.cat) combines the best in old- and new-technology rides, offering spectacular views from its perfect perch on a 542m (1,778ft) peak.

AROUND BARCELONA

MONTSERRAT

Just 40km (25 miles) northwest of Barcelona, and easily reached by train and cable car, the monastery of **Montserrat** ❾ sits on the ridge of a highly unusual rock formation 1,135m (3,725ft) above the Llobregat river valley. This is the spiritual home of Catalunya and one of Spain's most important pilgrimage sites thanks to the monastery's Black Madonna – *La Moreneta* – a statue said to have been made by St Luke and brought to Barcelona by St Peter. In 1808, Napoleon's troops destroyed the original 12th-century monastery and the present building dates from 1874.

Montserrat (www.abadiamontserrat.cat) is an active Benedictine monastery; visitors may only enter the beautiful Gothic cloister, the basilica, and the museum. A highlight of any visit is a recital by the famous Escolania Boys' Choir (Mon–Fri at 1pm, Sun at noon and 6.45pm except Jul–Aug; www.escolania.cat), while the **museum** features art by El Greco, Picasso and modern Catalan artists, as well as interesting archaeological treasures. It is easy to escape the crowds by following one of the four well-signposted hermitage walks through Montserrat's magnificent protected mountain parkland. One of these leads to the **Santa Cova** (the Holy Cave) where *La Moreneta* was allegedly discovered.

POBLET

Travel 133km (83 miles) west of Barcelona to find the **Monestir de Poblet** ⑩, the largest and best-preserved Cistercian monastery in Europe (daily 10am–12.30pm and 3–5.30pm; www.poblet.cat). The monastery was founded in 1151 by Ramon Berenguer, the Count of Barcelona, as a gesture of thanksgiving for the reconquest of Catalunya. Poblet's facade is a majestic sight, and once inside the tour leads past the wine cellars, library, chapter house and refectory into the Romanesque and Gothic-style church and its spacious rose-garden cloister.

INLAND ANDALUCÍA

Andalucía is the southernmost autonomous region of Spain, stretching from the Atlantic and Portuguese border in the west to the Mediterranean south of Murcia in the east. It consists of eight provinces: Huelva, Cádiz, Málaga, Granada, Almería, Seville, Córdoba and Jaén. It has a magnificent array of scenery, including the Sierra Nevada – the highest peaks in mainland Spain – the alluvial plains of the Guadalquivir river, the deserts of Almería and the *pueblos blancos* (white villages) of the interior. Epitomised by its bullfighting and flamenco dancing, Andalucía is considered by many to be the soul of Spain. Its face has been moulded by both Spanish and Arabic cultures, and the fascinating mix can be found all over the region.

SEVILLE

When Julius Caesar arrived in Spain in 45bc, **Seville** (Sevilla) ⑪ was a thriving riverside settlement, but under the Romans it became a major town. Two Roman emperors – Hadrian and Trajan – were born in nearby Itálica. Subsequently capital of the Visigoths and then of a Moorish *taifa*, Seville finally fell to King Fernando III in 1248. A monopoly on trade with the New World brought the city to its peak during the Golden Age. 'Madrid is the capital of Spain,' the saying went, 'but Seville is the capital of the world.' Without doubt, the beautiful capital of Andalucía and Spain's fourth largest city is the most important city in the region. Its name is evocative of bullfighting, flamenco, the operatic temptress Carmen and many icons that represent Spain in visitors' minds.

The city's two most prominent monuments are located around the Plaza del Triunfo. The **cathedral** (Mon 11am–3.30pm, Tue–Sat 11am–5pm, Sun 2.30–6pm; charge includes entry to the Giralda tower; Mon 4.30–6pm free audio guide if booked in advance; www.catedraldeseville.es) is the largest Gothic church in the world, and among cathedrals is only surpassed in size by St Peter's in Rome and St Paul's in London. It was begun in 1401 after the great mosque was razed and completed in just over a century. The new building followed the ground plan of the old mosque, accounting for its unusual broad, rectangular form. Massive without, and richly decorated within, the cathedral contains more than 30 chapels, including the central **Capilla Mayor** with its Flemish

Plateresque altarpiece, and the **Capilla Real** (Royal Chapel), last resting place of Fernando III, the 'King-Saint' who delivered Seville from the hands of the infidel. The stunning altar screen is overlaid with 3,500kg (7,716lb) of gold. Christopher Columbus (Cristobal Colón) is interred in the 19th-century sarcophagus by the south entrance. His remains were transferred to Seville from Havana in 1898, when Cuba won its independence from Spain.

On the north side of the cathedral is the **Patio de los Naranjos** (Court of the Orange Trees), the ceremonial courtyard of the old mosque with its original ablutions fountains. The bell tower of the cathedral, the celebrated **Giralda** tower – Sevilla's most famous landmark – dates from 1184, and was the original mosque's minaret. The exterior is decorated with typical *sebka* design work, while the interior has a series of 35 gently rising ramps (designed for horses to climb – Fernando

Fusion of Moorish and Christian elements at Seville's Alcázar

III rode his horse to the top following the Reconquest in 1248) leading to an observation platform 70m (230ft) in the air and offering a tremendous panorama across the city.

The **Alcázar** is a major monument of mid-14th century Mudéjar architecture, combining Moorish, Gothic and Renaissance elements (Apr–Sept daily 9.30am–7pm, Oct–Mar daily 9.30am–5pm; night visits Apr–Sept 9–10.30pm, Oct 7.30–9pm; free last hour on Mon; www.alcazarseville.org). Built by Moorish craftsmen under Christian rule, during the reign of Pedro the Cruel, the rambling palace and its several courtyards incorporate fragments of an earlier Moorish fortress, and blend Christian motifs with Moorish designs. Not to be missed are the extensive and beautiful gardens, an oasis of tranquillity in this perpetually busy city.

Enjoying drinks under the watchful eye of the Giralda tower

Bordering the Alcázar, the labyrinthine streets of the **Barrio de Santa Cruz** exude history and charm. On the border of this district, more Mudéjar sensations await in the 16th-century **Casa de Pilatos** (daily 9am–6pm, Apr–Oct until 7pm; www.fundacionmedinaceli.org).

On the banks of the river is another of Seville's icons. The Moorish **Torre del Oro** (Tower of Gold) is named after the gold-coloured tiles that once covered the walls of this early 13th-century tower

– all that remains of Seville's medieval fortifications.

Other places not to miss are the **Hospital de la Caridad** (Charity Hospital), the **Plaza de España**, the **Bullfighting Museum and Plaza de Toros**, the **Museo de Bellas Artes** (Tue–Sat 9am–7.30pm, Sun 9am–3.30pm, June–Sept Tue–Sun 9am–3.30pm; free for EU citizens; www.museode bellasartesdeseville.es) with its impressive art collection, and the site of Roman **Itálica**, 10km (6 miles) to the northwest.

> ## Colourful mosaic
>
> The colourful glazed ceramic tiles *(azulejos)* that you see in Seville owe their origins to the Moors, who adorned their palaces with mosaics in sophisticated geometric patterns. (The word *azulejo* derives from the Arabic for 'little stone'.)

CÓRDOBA

Córdoba ⑫ was the largest city in Roman Spain, the capital of the province of Baetica, and birthplace of Seneca the Younger, philosopher and tragedian. But its golden era was between the mid-8th and very early 11th centuries, when it was the centre of the great medieval Caliphate of Córdoba. As one of the world's largest and most cultured cities, the splendid capital of the western Islamic Empire had the first university and the earliest street lighting in Europe.

The city is dominated by the greatest surviving monument from that period, the breathtaking Great Mosque known as **La Mezquita** (Mon–Sat 10am–7pm, Sun 8.30–11.30am and 3–7pm, daily until 6pm in winter, night visits Mon–Sat in summer; free Mon–Sat 8.30–9.30; www.catedraldecordoba.es). Begun in 786, it was enlarged three times before attaining its present size, covering an area of 2 hectares (5 acres) in 987. Córdoba was reconquered in 1236, and two small Christian chapels were added in 1258 and 1260. In the early 16th century Carlos V constructed a Christian cathedral in the centre of the mosque.

Inside La Mezquita, Córdoba

With heavy ornamentation, a blaze of colour and human images in paint, stone and wood, it contrasts shockingly with the understated simplicity of Islamic design. Set in the southeast wall is the splendid 10th-century **mihrab** (the niche pointing towards Mecca) lined with marble and gold mosaics, and the **maksourah**, the enclosure where the caliph attended to his prayers.

A Christian king, Alfonso XI, built Córdoba's **Alcázar de los Reyes Cristianos** (Tue–Sat 8.30am–3pm, Sun 9.30am–2.30pm, with show ticket Mon–Sat 3–9pm, Sun 2.30–9pm; www.alcazardelosreyes cristianos.cordoba.es), where you'll find patios, Roman relics, terraced gardens, and ramparts with fine views. Fernando and Isabel received Columbus and planned the invasion of Granada while they were in residence here.

Also well worth a visit are the 14th-century **synagogue** in the **Barrio de la Judería** (Jewish Quarter), the 16th-century **Palacio de los Marquéses de Viana**, with 13 flower-filled patios that are so typical of Córdoba, the **Plaza de la Corredera** dating from the 17th century and the only Castilian-style plaza in Andalucía, the **Museo Arqueológico** and the **Museo Taurino**. Look, also, for the unusual Plaza del Potro, home to the **Museo Diocesano de Bellas Artes** (Fine Arts Museum) and the **Museo Julio Romero de Torres**.

MEDINA AZAHARA

Eight kilometres (5 miles) west of Córdoba are the ruins of the intriguing Medina Azahara city-palace, commissioned in 936 by Abdel-Rahman III in honour of his favourite concubine Al Zahra (The Flower). It had a short life because it was razed with the breakup of the Caliphate of Córdoba in the early 11th century. For nearly 900 years it was left in ruins, and not until 1910 did the slow work of excavating begin. Excavation still continues, but reconstructed **royal apartments** give some impression of the original magnificence of this sumptuous complex of baths, schools, gardens and stately apartments built on three terraces.

GRANADA

The Nasrid dynasty rose to power in **Granada** ⑬ just as the fortunes of the Spanish Moors were beginning to wane, when Mohammed ben Alhamar established his capital here in 1232, after Fernando III had forced him from Jaén. Two years later, Moors fleeing from the newly vanquished Seville swelled the population, which had already been augmented by refugees from Córdoba. These industrious Moors set about making Granada the grandest city of Andalucía, creating the sumptuous hilltop palace of the Alhambra. Granada was the last of the great Moorish kingdoms of Andalucía to be reconquered, having survived more than 250 years longer than the others. King Boabdil's surrender to the Catholic Monarchs in January 1492 marked the end of the Muslim Empire in Spain.

One of the most visited monuments in Spain, the world-famous **Alhambra** (meaning 'The Red') takes its name from the red-brown bricks used in the construction of its outer walls (8.30am–8pm, until 6pm in winter; night visits: summer Tue–Sat 10–11.30pm, winter Fri–Sat 8–9.30pm; www.alhambra-patronato.es). Rising precipitously above the deep

The Alhambra, with the peaks of the Sierra Nevada in the background

gorge of the River Darro, it has the towering – and often snow-covered – peaks of the Sierra Nevada as a backdrop.

There are four main areas to explore at the Alhambra: the Alcazaba, Palacios Nazaríes, Palacio de Carlos V and the Generalife. The Alcazaba (fortress) is the oldest section, with towers dating back to the mid-13th century. From the top of the **Torre de la Vela** (Watchtower) there are excellent views over the modern city below. The Nazrid Palaces lie at the heart of the Alhambra. The intricacy and bountiful beauty of the designs here create a visual impression that is beyond mere words.

The highlights are the **Salón de Embajadores** (Hall of the Ambassadors), or royal audience chamber, one of the most sumptuously ornamented rooms in the Alhambra; the **Patio de los Leones**, the name of which derives from the splashing fountain in the centre upheld by 12 stone lions; the **Torre de las Damas** (Tower of the Ladies), and the old bathing area.

The **Palacio de Carlos V** was commissioned in 1527 by Carlos V; square on the outside, it has a surprisingly elegant two-storey circular patio inside. The palace houses the **Museo de la Alhambra** (same hours as La Alhambra) and the **Museo de Bellas Artes** (Fine Arts Museum).

The **Generalife**, at the eastern end of the Alhambra fortifications, is a modest summer palace surrounded by beautiful terraced gardens, where oleander and roses bloom luxuriantly, and delicate fountains play among the neatly clipped cypress hedges.

Facing the Alhambra hill, the **Albaicín**, Granada's oldest and most picturesque quarter, is fun to explore, affording glimpses of the Alhambra between whitewashed houses, outdoor restaurants and cafés. At the bottom of the hill are some Arab baths.

Down in the city is the exquisite Renaissance **Capilla Real** (Royal Chapel; www.capillarealgranada.com), that serves as the mausoleum of the Catholic Monarchs, as well as their daughter, Juana La Loca, and her husband, Felipe El Hermoso. Their mortal remains were interred in the crypt below in 1521, after a ceremonial transfer from the Alhambra. On show in the **sacristy**

VISITING THE ALHAMBRA

To protect the Alhambra, admission numbers are controlled. Tickets are limited and sold according to availability. You can avoid queuing or disappointment if you book in advance (minimum one day, maximum one year ahead) through any branch of La Caixa bank, by telephoning 902 888 001, or online at www.alhambra-tickets.es. You pay by credit card, are given a code number and collect your tickets from the Alhambra ticket office. Note that you are given a time slot to visit the Palacios Nazaríes and you must enter within it.

(Mon–Sat 10.15am–1.30pm, 4–7.30pm, Sun 11am–1.30pm, 2.30–6.30pm, winter until 6.30pm; free Nov–Feb) are mementos of them, including Fernando's sword and Isabel's sceptre and crown, a circle of gold embellished with acanthus scrolls.

JEREZ DE LA FRONTERA

The largest city in the province of Cádiz, **Jerez** ⑭ enjoys a fame based upon sherry and horses. The English corrupted Jerez to 'sherry' and exported the locally produced wine. Several of the many *bodegas* in Jerez offer free tastings. As for the horses, the **Real Escuela Andaluza del Arte Ecuestre** (Royal Andalucían School of Equestrian Art; www.realescuela.org) puts its star pupils through a beautifully choreographed dressage show at noon (Tue and Thu, Aug–Sept also Fri), and there are weekday training sessions and sometimes special galas. The highlight of the equestrian calendar is the May Spring Horse Fair, when the town is full of horses and their elaborately dressed riders.

A famous name in Jerez

An 11th-century mosque is found inside the **Alcázar fortress**, and the nearby 18th-century Colegiata holds a precious image of Christ of the Vineyards. Among the other attractions, look especially for the **Museo de**

Arte Flamenco in the distinguished Palacio de Penmartin and the **Clock Museum** in La Atalaya Palace.

CARMONA

Carmona has a history that dates back to the neolithic period 5,000 years ago. It was the Roman era, though, that brought the area prosperity and wealth, and the **Museo y Necropolis** (June–mid-Sept daily 9am–3.30pm) is the largest Roman necropolis outside Rome, boasting an extraordinary number of palaces, mansions, convents and churches. It also has two formidable gates that stood on the old *card maxim* (the Roman road).

RONDA

Dramatically clinging to a cliff-top 150m (500ft) above the Tajo Gorge, **Ronda** ⓰ was an Iberian then a Roman settlement. Under the Moors it proved impregnable for seven centuries. The **Puente Nuevo** spans the gorge and connects the new centre with the old town, from where Ronda's Moorish kings and its Christian conquerors ruled from the **Palacio de Mondragón**. Behind a Renaissance portal, the elegant courtyards, horseshoe arches and Arabic inscriptions reveal the origins of this stately structure that now houses the town museum. The town's former main mosque survives a short walk away as the **Santa María la Mayor** church.

Back across the bridge, seek out the perfect neoclassical **Plaza de Toros** (bullring), one of the oldest in Spain and venerated as the cradle of the *corrida* as it is staged today (see page 139). It was a Ronda man, Francisco Romero, who spelled out the rules of bullfighting in the 18th century. There's a small museum here that is of interest to the non-aficionado.

THE WHITE TOWNS

Andalucía is at its most picturesque in the brilliant white-washed villages and towns *(pueblos blancos)* that dot the mountains between Málaga and Cádiz. Many of them are spectacularly located high on hillsides or under the walls of crumbling castles. All are higgledy-piggledy labyrinths of tapering streets, steps and shady alleyways which have changed little since they were inhabited by Spain's Moorish population in the middle ages. The best known of them is Ronda. Two other good bases for exploring the area are **Arcos de la Frontera** and **Grazalema**. Perhaps the prettiest of the white towns is **Zahara de la Sierra**.

Zahara de la Sierra

BAEZA, ÚBEDA AND JAÉN

The beautifully preserved twin towns of Baeza and Úbeda in the province of Jaén flourished as Christian strongholds during the Reconquest. **Baeza**, with more than 50 listed historical buildings, is the smaller of the two. **Úbeda** is just as engaging, and its showcase square, the **Plaza Vázquez de Molina**, is surrounded by a host of magnificent Renaissance palaces and churches. The town hall is housed in the **Palacio de las Cadenas** (Palace of Chains), so called for the chains round its forecourt, and the stunningly rich domed **Sacra Capilla del Salvador** is the town's finest church. The **Hospital de Santiago**, designed by Andrés de Vandelvira, with its Renaissance courtyard, is another gem.

Surrounded by millions of olive trees, the provincial capital **Jaén** ⑯ is known as the 'world capital of olive oil'. Its enormous Renaisance **cathedral**, the **Baños Arabes** (Arab baths) and the **Museo Provincial** are well worth a visit, as is the Arab **Castillo de Santa Catalina** which overlooks the city.

Away to the east, the limestone ridges and deep valleys of the **Parque Natural de las Sierras de Cazorla, Segura y las Villas** comprise Spain's largest nature-and-game reserve.

THE COSTAS

From the Costa Brava at the eastern end of the Pyrenees all the way round to the Costa de la Luz and the border with Portugal, the famous Spanish *costas* attract millions of holidaymakers every year. The coastline stretches for some 2,500km (1,562 miles) from the sheltered Mediterranean to the blustery Atlantic and is extremely varied. There are rocky coves and glorious stretches of golden sand, family resorts and jet-set ports. In spite of the much-reported ravages caused by extensive building you can still find many charming spots along the coast.

COSTA BRAVA

Stretching from the French border to just north of Barcelona, this is perhaps the prettiest coastline in Spain. The cliffs and coves of the 'Wild Coast' still conceal a handful of traditional fishing villages and secluded beaches in the north of the region. You will find the major tourism development concentrated in the south (at Lloret de Mar, for instance).

Cadaqués ⑰ may look like a typical whitewashed fishermen's village, but it attracts a crowd of chic, monied holidaymakers. Although it is still a working port, without a decent beach, the village has developed into something of an artists' haunt. In fact, Salvador Dalí built a modest retreat here on the edge of Cadaqués at Port Lligat in 1929. The bizarre house that he and his wife Gala created out of a series of fishermen's cottages is now open to the public as the **Casa-Museu Salvador Dalí** (same opening hours as Figueras, see box). Visitor numbers are strictly controlled and prior booking is essential.

Empúries was built by the Greeks, improved by the Iberians, and then greatly expanded by the Romans. The site was perpetually occupied for some 1,500 years. Excavations have uncovered the remains of the villas, temples and marketplaces of these different civilisations. You will also find lovely sea views. The most sensational find was a statue of

DALÍ IN FIGUERES

Born in Figueres (Figueras), 30km (19 miles) west of Cadaqués, in 1904, the Surrealist artist Salvador Dalí endowed his home town with the suitably surreal **Teatre-Museu Dalí** (July–Sept daily 9am–8pm, Oct Tue–Sun 9.30am–6pm, Nov–Feb Tue–Sun 10.30am–6pm, Mar–June Tue–Sun 9.30am–6pm, night visits Aug 10pm–1am; www. salvador-dali.org). The second most visited museum in Spain (after the Prado), it is a typically outrageous Dalíesque project. A municipal theatre was gutted, its stage filled with bizarre sculptures, and an ancient Cadillac supporting a statue of a gilt-breasted Amazon was parked on the patio. There are giant models of hens' eggs on the battlements, a roofline topped by a geodesic dome, and Dalí's version of the Sistine Chapel – a homage to Mae West, with her lips replaced by a voluptuous red sofa. Shocks and humour aside, the museum represents an intriguing cross-section of Dalí's work.

Popular Tossa de Mar on the Costa Brava

Asclepius, the Greek god of medicine, which was sculpted in marble from an Athenian quarry. The original has been removed to Barcelona, but a copy stands in the ruined temple. The on-site **museum** (www.mac.cat) displays local finds, from ceramics and jewels to household items and weapons.

The **Medes Islands** off the brash resort of L'Estartit are a nature reserve popular with snorkellers and scuba divers. You can also sail around on a glass-bottom boat.

The most scenic and unspoilt stretch of the Costa Brava is from Begur to Tossa de Mar, a series of cliffs punctuated by coves concealing pretty beaches, such as those of **Aigua Blava**, **Sa Tuna**, **Tamariu Llafranc** and **Calella de Palafrugell**. **Tossa de Mar** itself was an artists' colony before it metamorphosed into a fully developed international resort. The town remains surprisingly attractive, its **Vila Vella** (Old Town) enclosed by brooding 12th-century walls and guarded by three great towers. The **museum** here contains paintings by Marc Chagall and works by other artists who visited the town.

Girona **⑱** is the capital of the Costa Brava, and is a pleasant day-trip destination from the coast 30km (20 miles) west. The old town is fun to explore, with its typical medieval streets such as **Carrer de la Força**, once the heart of the Jewish quarter. Girona's Gothic **cathedral** (www.catedral degirona.org) is said to have the widest nave in the world at 22m (72ft), and the treasury, the **Museu Capitular**, is crammed with precious gold and silverwork, rare illuminated manuscripts, statuary and an extraordinary 11th-century tapestry of the Creation. The 12th-century **Banys Arabs** (Arab Baths) nearby are not Arabic at all, but they are intriguing nevertheless.

COSTA DAURADA

Stretching from just south of Barcelona to the Ebro Delta, the Costa Daurada derives its name from the fine golden

The beach at Sitges

(*daurada*) sand beaches that stretch almost without a break for 241km (150 miles).

Sitges ⑲, a sophisticated and attractive resort, popular with young weekenders from Barcelona, retains much of its old-world charm and the old town is built around a promontory. Here stands the **Museu Maricel** (Tue–Sun 10am–8pm, Mar–Jun and Oct until 7pm, Nov–Feb 10am–5pm; www.museusdesitges. com), which houses a fine collection of paintings and *objets d'art* from around the world, and offers romantic sea views through picture windows. Adjacent **Cau Ferrat** (same opening hours) houses one of Spain's most exquisite small museums. Works by El Greco and Picasso, ceramics, crystal and much more are imaginatively displayed. Another good museum is the **Museu Romàntic** (closed for restoration), situated in an aristo-cratic mansion lavishly decorated in 19th-century style.

TARRAGONA AND BEYOND

Tarragona ⑳, 95km (60 miles) south of Barcelona, was the site of an ancient Iberian settlement, but it was the Romans, in the 3rd century BC, who established it as an important military and political base. Tarraco, as it was then known, quickly grew to a population of 30,000 and minted its own cur-rency. By 27BC it was the capital of Tarraconensis, the largest Roman province on the Iberian peninsula. The town now has some of the finest Roman remains to have survived in Spain.

The Rambla Vella (Old Rambla) neatly divides Tarragona in half. To the north is the old walled city, while to the south is the Rambla Nova (New Rambla) and the modern part of town. At the end of the Rambla Vella the **Balcó del Mediterrani** looks down onto Tarragona's commercial port, one of the busiest in the Mediterranean and teeming with fish restaurants.

To get a glimpse of the old city, you can take a walk along the **Passeig Arqueològic**. This follows the top of the old city

Tarragona's Roman amphitheatre, built into the hillside

walls, which enclose a maze of charming medieval streets. The upper levels of the ramparts were built by the Romans above huge cyclopean boulders, supposedly placed there by Iberian tribes in the 6th century BC. In this part of town, the **Museu Arqueològic** (www.mnat.cat) in Plaça del Rei has a modern, well-designed exhibition of delicate mosaics and other ancient artefacts. Next door, the **Pretori Romà** (Roman Praetorium) is thought to have been part of the original complex belonging to the provincial administration. It was restored in the Middle Ages and today houses the atmospheric **Museu d'Història** (History Museum). Walking from here towards the sea brings you to the ruins of both the Roman **amphitheatre**, where gladiators once fought, built into the hillside, and the 12th-century **Santa María del Miracle** church.

Medieval Tarragona's pride and joy is its **cathedral**, the largest in Catalunya, founded in 1171 but not consecrated until 1333. The 12th- to 13th-century cloister is an attraction in its own right, while the **Museu Diocesà** (http://museu.

diocesa.arquebisbattarragona.cat) has a fine collection of art treasures and Flemish tapestries.

Beyond the old city walls is the **Necròpolis i Museu Paleocristiàns** (Necropolis and Paleo-Christian Museum; www.mnat.cat), which stands at the site of the city's early Christian burial ground. Excavations have uncovered more than 2,000 graves; you will find the best archaeological discoveries displayed in the museum.

Tarragona's most impressive Roman monument, the first-century **Pont del Diable**, is some 4km (2.5 miles) north of the town centre, off the N240 towards Lleida (Lérida). The 'Devil's Bridge' is actually a perfectly preserved two-storey aqueduct, which spans 217m (712ft) and rises to a height of 27m (88ft) above the ground.

Just south of Tarragona, **Salou** is by far the biggest resort on the Costa Daurada. It is a well-ordered, no-frills playground for north European package tourists, offering them extensive beaches and a good range of facilities and entertainment. Salou also has a huge theme park, **Port Aventura** (www.portaventura.es), which promises a journey of adventure through exotic lands, plus all sorts of rides, restaurants and live entertainment. On summer evenings, crowds assemble to watch the town's **illuminated fountain**, which was designed by Carlos Buigas, better known for the famous 'Magic Fountains' in Barcelona.

Cambrils, Salou's more classy neighbour, is an attractive fishing port turned resort that has a long seafront and a charming oddity in its large fleet of *bous* – small boats that carry outsize lamps when they go out to fish at night.

EBRO DELTA

The **Ebro Delta** ㉑ is the largest of Catalunya's wetlands and, after France's Camargue, the most important aquatic environment in the western Mediterranean. It is a major breeding ground for waders, waterfowl and sea birds. A large area of the delta wetlands has been set aside as a protected National Park, making this a true birdwatcher's paradise. The tourist office at **Deltebre** can supply general information, maps, and details of boat excursions and birdwatching sites. Non-birdwatchers can enjoy the wide open spaces, the glittering green rice paddies (the basic ingredient for *paella* is grown here) and glimpses of the sleepy rural lifestyle.

Tortosa held a key strategic role for centuries as the last major town before the sea. Guarding the Ebro river, the **La Zuda** fortress at the top of the town was constructed by the Moors, who held out at length here during the 1148 Reconquest. Later it became a royal residence of the Aragonese kings; today it houses a *parador*. The **cathedral** in the old town was built between the 14th and 16th centuries, and is a fine example

Picturesque Peñíscola

of Catalan Gothic architecture. Inside, do not miss the 14th-century triptych or the two 15th-century carved stone pulpits.

COSTA DEL AZAHAR

The 'Orange Blossom Coast' begins south of the Ebro Delta and stretches south towards Valencia for 100km (60 miles) down a section of coast that is well endowed with beaches backed by olive orchards and the citrus groves after which the coast is named.

Peñíscola ㉒, picturesque and crowned by a medieval castle, is built on a rocky promontory. The **castle** (daily 10.30am–5.30pm, summer 9.30am–9.30pm) built by the Knights Templar on the ruins of a Moorish fortress, has two claims to fame: Pope Benedict XIII found asylum here after being dismissed from his position until his death in 1423, and it featured in the film *El Cid*, starring Charlton Heston. There's a museum and terrific sea views from the ramparts.

Sagunto (Roman Saguntum) underwent a nine-month siege by the Carthaginian general Hannibal in 219BC that ignited the Second Punic War. The inhabitants set fire to the city and killed themselves to avoid capture, but when Saguntum was eventually retaken, the Romans redeveloped it on a grand scale. Today, Sagunto's principal Roman monument is the heavily restored 2nd-century **amphitheatre**. Nearby is a modest **archaeological museum** with Iberian, Roman and medieval relics. From the hilltop acropolis, **Castell de Sagunt**, there are sweeping views over the citrus orchards to the sea.

VALENCIA

Founded by the Romans in 138BC, **Valencia ㉓** later prospered as the capital of a far-flung Moorish kingdom until El Cid briefly recaptured it at the end of the 11th century. In 1238 Jaime I, El Conquistador (whose banner and sword can be seen in the

The Gothic El Micalet, a symbol of Valencia

Museo Historico Municipal), reconquered the city and proclaimed the Kingdom of Valencia. Today, Valencia is Spain's third largest city and most of its monuments are within the area bounded by the Turia Gardens (once a river) and the railway station.

The **cathedral** (Mon–Sat 10am–6.30pm, Sun 2–6.30pm, winter Mon–Sat until 5.30pm, closed Sun 2–5pm; www. catedraldevalencia.es) was started in 1262 on the site of a Moorish mosque but it is a mix of styles, with most parts dating from the 14th–15th centuries. The octagonal Gothic tower is known as **El Micalet**, and you can climb the 207 steps to the top for spectacular views. A chapel contains what is said to be the Holy Grail.

Valencia is surrounded by more than 930 hectares (2,300 acres) of irrigated land *(huerta)* and for over 1,000 years disputes have been settled by the Tribunal de Aguas (Water Council). This is a group of eight men who meet every Thursday at midday outside the Door of the Apostles of the cathedral. Business is conducted verbally in Valenciano (the local language).

Valencia's **La Lonja** (Silk Exchange; Tue–Sat 9.30am–7pm, Sun 9.30am–2pm; free Sun; www.museosymonumentos valencia.com) dates from the late 15th century. Besides being one of the finest secular Gothic structures in Europe it is also famous for its **Hall of Pillars** where finely crafted helicoidal columns curve graciously to the roof. Across the street the

Modernist-style **central market** (daily until 3pm; www.mercado centralvalencia.es), built between 1910 and 1926, is an irregular eight-sided iron girder and glass building where you will find an enticing array of meat, fish, vegetables and fruit. Outside, look for stalls that sell *paella* pans in a huge range of sizes.

The **Museo Nacional de Cerámica** (Tue–Sat 10am–2pm and 4–8pm, Sun 10am–2pm; free Sat pm and Sun; www.mecd.gob. es/mnceramica), housed in the astonishing Palacio del Marqués de Dos Aguas, is a gem of a museum and among its treasures it has hundreds of glorious glazed tiles *(azulejos)* for which the city is famous. The city's major art collection, at the **Museo de Bellas Artes** (Mon 11am–5pm, Tue–Sun 10am–7pm; free; http://museobellasartes valencia.gva.es), has paintings by Bosch, El Greco, Goya and Velázquez, and a definitive collection of 15th-century Valencian art.

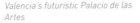

Valencia's futuristic Palacio de las Artes

The **Serrano** and **Quart** towers are formidable reminders that such defensive fortifications were vital in centuries past. The **Institut Valencià d'Art Modern** (IVAM; Tue–Sun noon–8.30pm; www. ivam.es) has an interesting collection of 20th-century art, notably by Paul Klee, Francis Picabia, Robert Rauschenberg and Constantin Brancusi.

Ninots

Artists and craftsmen work all year to create the elaborate *ninots* – papier-mâché figures that are set alight at the climax of Valencia's Las Fallas festival in March. Those figures voted too good for burning are saved from the flames and exhibited in the Museu Faller (www.fallas.com).

Just outside the city centre is the futuristic **Ciudad de las Artes y las Ciencias** (Arts and Sciences Park; www.cac.es; Mon–Fri 9am–8pm, Sat 10am–8pm, Sun 10am–3pm), a complex of buildings and parklands dedicated to fun and learning. **L'Hemisfèric**, an IMAX cinema and planetarium built in the shape of a gigantic open eye, was designed by Valencian architect Santiago Calatrava. Other attractions are the **Palacio de las Artes**, a concert hall with a huge open-air auditorium, the **Museo de las Ciencias** (Science Museum), also designed by Calatrava, and the **Parque Oceanográfico**, an underwater city and aquarium with killer whales and dolphins.

COSTA BLANCA

The Costa Blanca, which begins to the south of Valencia, was named Akra Leuka ('White Headland') by ancient Greek tradesmen who founded a colony here 2,500 years ago. The hot, dry climate, brilliant light and miles of fine, sandy beaches and temperate water make the 'White Coast' one of Spain's liveliest tourist zones.

A town in two parts, **Gandía** has a busy resort on a vast beach down on the coast and a fine 14th-century palace tucked away in its inland town centre. Birthplace of Duke Francisco de Borja, 16th-century noble turned Jesuit priest, the **Palacio Ducal** (www.palauducal.com) is now a showcase for splendid tapestries, paintings and antiques, many of them amassed by the pious duke.

Beyond Gandía, the town of **Dénia** is named after a Roman temple dedicated to the goddess Diana. Further south, the resort of **Jávea** (Xàbia) has a fine beach and a pleasant old quarter. **Calpe** (Calp) is a former fishing village with pleasant sandy beaches in the lee of the **Peñón de Ifach**, an imposing volcanic outcrop. **Altea's** old houses climb steeply to a carefully preserved old quarter, home to a thriving artistic community.

Benidorm used to symbolise the worst excesses of package tourism. It has a towering skyline that stretches back from the 7km (4-mile) beach, and provides what holiday makers want – sunshine, beaches, bars and entertainment. Surprisingly, the old fishermen's quarter still exists, and there are sweeping views from the attractive **Balcón del Mediterráneo**. Boats visit the **Isla de Benidorm**, an offshore bird sanctuary. Adding to its attractions, the **Terra Mítica** theme park (www.terramiticapark.com) has state-of-the-art technology intended to take visitors on a journey through the history of the lost ancient civilisations of the Mediterranean.

Castell de Guadalest

The Moorish eagles' nest village-fortress **Castell de Guadalest**, situated 28km (17 miles) northwest, is a favourite excursion.

Alicante ㉔ (Alicant) is a bustling Mediterranean port with a splendid palm-lined

Along Alicante's promenade

promenade, lots of outdoor cafés and the spacious beach of **Playa Postiguet**. Its imposing cliff-top **Castillo de Santa Bárbara** was built on the site of a Carthaginian fort founded in the 3rd century BC. Below the castle, the old **Barrio de Cruz** is atmospheric and full of character. Here you will find the baroque facade of the 14th-century church of **Santa María** next to the **Museo de Arte Contemporáneo de Alicante** (MACA; www.maca-alicante. es), focusing on the Spanish artists Miró, Picasso and Dalí.

Elche (Elx), situated a little way inland, is famous for its palm plantations. The **Palacio de Altamira**, a former royal holiday residence, is now occupied by an archaeological museum that has a replica of the famous *Dama de Elche* sculpture, which dates from the 5th century bc (the original is in Madrid).

The most famous stretch of the Costa Cálida, which forms the southern part of the Costa Blanca, is the **Mar Menor** (Little Sea), a vast lagoon almost completely sheltered from the Mediterranean by a 22km (14-mile) spit. High-rise resort facilities have multiplied on the sandy breakwater, La Manga.

Cartagena, named after the Carthaginians, is an important port and naval base with a harbour overlooked by the ruins of the 14th-century **Castillo de la Concepción**.

Murcia, the inland capital of the province of the same name, which includes the Costa Cálida, is pleasant and prosperous, with a pretty old town. The 14th-century **Catedral de Santa María** is one of Spain's finest, adorned with a fabulous baroque facade. The Vélez chapel is a highlight of the interior, and in the museum there are wood sculptures by Francisco Salzillo (1707–83), Murcia's greatest artist. There are more of his works in the **Museo Salzillo** (www.museosalzillo.es). Of Murcia's other museums, the **Museo Provincial de Bellas Artes** (Fine Arts) is the best.

COSTA DE ALMERÍA

Almería ㉕ is a modern city that reveals its Moorish origins in the form of the gigantic 8th-century **Alcazaba fortress**, which overhangs the town and port. The city's crenellated outer walls and a section of the turreted ramparts remain standing among the 35 hectares (87 acres) of ruins. The arterial **Paseo de Almería** is ideal for strolling and shopping. Inland from the harbour, the fortified Gothic **cathedral** was completed in the mid-16th century.

Almería province is Spain's dustbowl – a parched corner of the coast, where development has been kept at bay until recently. There are the resorts of **Mojácar**, **Roquetas de Mar** and **Garrucha**, while inland the dramatic, desolate landscape was a favourite with Western film-makers, who nicknamed it **Mini-Hollywood**.

COSTA TROPICAL

The coastline of the province of Granada is the most attractive, and the least developed, part of Spain's southern coast. There are no large developments and few hotels, just numerous uncrowded small beaches with crystal clear water, surrounded by the mountains sloping down to the sea.

Almuñécar is the only holiday resort of any size, and it has an ancient history. A fine aqueduct stands as a monument to the skills of the Roman engineers who constructed it during the reign of Antoninus Pius in the 2nd century ad. **Salobreña**, just to the west, is a town of whitewashed houses clinging to the slopes of a rocky, cone-shaped hill that is crowned with a magnificent Moorish castle.

COSTA DEL SOL

Nerja marks the eastern end of the Costa del Sol. Its cliff-top **Balcón de Europa** has a lovely palm-fringed promenade. The main attraction is the **Cueva de Nerja**, (www.cuevadenerja. es) a truly cavernous grotto 4km (2.5 miles) east of town. Wall paintings and archaeological finds indicate that the stalactite-encrusted cave – home to the world's longest stalactite at 59m (195ft) – has been inhabited since the days of Cro-Magnon man.

Málaga ㉖ is the international gateway to the Costa del Sol, with many millions arriving at its airport every year. It also has a busy harbour overlooked by an **Alcazaba** (Apr–Oct 9am–8pm, Nov–Mar 9am–6pm) built by the Moors, now consisting mostly of landscaped ruins with a modest archaeological museum. At the top of the hill, the sprawling **Gibralfaro** fort ruins (daily summer 9am–8pm, winter until 6pm) afford spectacular views out to sea and inland to the mountains. A short distance from Málaga's grandiose but gloomy cathedral in the bustling pedestrianised commercial centre is the **Museo Picasso**. Some 200 of his paintings, drawings, sculptures and ceramics fill the 16th-century Buenavista Palace (July–Aug daily 10am–8pm, Mar–June and Sept–Oct until 7pm, Nov–Feb until 6pm; free Sun last two hours; www.museopicassomalaga.org). Picasso was born

Málaga's pedestrianised Calle Marques de Larios

nearby at Plaza de la Merced 15, which is now the **Museo Casa Natal** of the Fundación Picasso (daily 9.30am–8pm; Nov–Mar closed Tue; free Sun; http://fundacionpicasso. malaga.eu). Once only really famous for its Picasso connection, Málaga has reinvented itself as an artistic hub with four other great museums: the **Centre Pompidou Málaga** (daily 9.30am–8pm, summer until 11pm; http://centrepompidou-malaga.eu), the **Centro de Arte Contemporáneo de Málaga CAC** (http://cacmalaga.eu), the **Museo Carmen Thyssen Málaga** (www.carmenthyssenmalaga.org), which hosts the biggest collection of 19th- and 20th-century Andalusian art, and the **Colección del Museo Ruso** (www.coleccionmuseo ruso.es), a vast Russian art collection.

Costumes and folk arts in the entertaining **Museo de Artes y Costumbres Populares**, in a 17th-century inn near the Guadalmedina riverbed, are worth a detour.

Torremolinos epitomises the popular side of the Costa del Sol, with tower-block hotels stretching well inland away from

Postcards for sale, Málaga

La Carihuela beach and its *chiringuitos* – small beach-side restaurants. The adjacent resort of **Fuengirola** is also popular, but more family-orientated.

Marbella, though, is the aristocrat of the Costa del Sol resorts, favoured by royalty and celebrities for decades. As a consequence, prices are higher here than anywhere else along the coast, but standards of accommodation and cuisine are superior, too. The 28km (17-mile) beachfront is built up with expensive hotel complexes, and the spacious marina sees more than its fair share of luxury pleasure craft. Across the main road, the old town is an attractive warren of streets and alleys full of shops, restaurants and the odd historic church.

Puerto Banús ㉗ is Spain's answer to St-Tropez. This chic 1970s marina-shopping-entertainment complex is full of tasteful bars, pricey boutiques, classy restaurants and night-clubs. Its waterfront parade is a catwalk for 'beautiful people', many of whom arrive aboard the massive yachts that are berthed in the harbour.

Estepona, although quite small, is the last of the resorts on the western flank of the coast. It provides all the essentials for a sporty, modern vacation – large luxury hotels, beaches, golf courses and a marina – all in an engaging ambiance. Of Roman origin, Estepona preserves the remains of Moorish fortifications and watchtowers.

THE COSTA DE LA LUZ

Stretching from the Strait of Gibraltar to the Portuguese border, the Atlantic-facing coast of southern Spain is aptly called the 'Coast of Light', because of the crystal clarity of its blue skies. Much loved by artists, it receives a mere trickle of tourists compared with its neighbour, the bustling Costa del Sol. It is extremely blustery and tourist facilities are limited, but to make up for that, there are long and uncrowded beaches, with easy access to Seville and to Spain's best national park, the Doñana (see box).

Tarifa, the windsurfing capital of Europe, is just 13km (8 miles) across the water from North Africa. Morocco's Rif mountains hang on the horizon, and Tangier is often clearly visible. Accomplished windsurfers revel in the strong and consistently windy conditions prevailing at **Tarifa beach**.

CÁDIZ

The ancient city of **Cádiz** ㉘, at the end of a very narrow peninsula of land running parallel to the coast, was founded by the

DOÑANA NATIONAL PARK

The largest and best known of Spain's national parks, this wild conservation zone, occupying the right bank of the Guadalquivir River at its estuary on the Atlantic Ocean, is the last great lowland wilderness in southern Europe. It has three distinct kinds of ecosystem: the *marismas* (salt marshes), the *matorral* (brushwood) and *las dunas* (the sand dunes). Within its boundaries can be found an amazing array of animal, bird and plant life, but what you see depends very much on the time of year. The best way see the park is by 4 x 4 bus tour from El Acebuche. For details see www.donanavisitas.es or tel: 959 430 432. Be warned, though, that this is a bumpy and rough ride.

Drake's damage

In 1587, English privateer Sir Francis Drake attacked the Spanish Armada as it lay at anchor in the Bay of Cádiz. Seizing some ships and burning others, he then razed the town before rampaging up and down the coast. His laconic comment, history records, was that he had 'singed the King of Spain's beard'.

Phoenicians in 1100bc and is considered to be Spain's oldest town. In fact, only the remains of the Roman theatre give much evidence of its age. Cádiz was reconquered by Alfonso X in 1262, granted the Monopoly of Trade with Africa by the Catholic Monarchs in 1493, and saw Columbus depart from here on his second and fourth voyages, in 1493 and 1502. In the latter part of the 16th century, the city twice came under attack by enemy naval forces. Just over a century later, a period of prosperity ensued when the Casa de Contratación, the monopoly rights for trade with the Americas, was transferred from Seville by order of Felipe V in 1717. A century later, on 19 March 1812, and while under attack from Napoleon's forces, the national parliament met in the St Felipe Neri church and proclaimed the first Spanish constitution.

The excellent **Museo de Cádiz** exhibits Phoenician and Roman artefacts and paintings by Francisco Zurbarán, as well as local crafts. Overlooking the ocean, the baroque and classical **cathedral** gives evidence of an extended construction period between 1772 and 1838, and has a landmark dome that glitters like gold in the sunshine. (The artist Murillo fell fatally from a scaffold when painting an altarpiece in 1816). The curious and unusual **Oratorio de la Santa Cueva** has underground chapels dating from 1783. Of more interest is the domed upper chapel added in 1796. Five spectacular paintings adorn its ceiling – three are fine examples of Goya's work.

SANLÚCAR DE BARRAMEDA

Situated at the mouth of the Guadalquivir River on the Atlantic coast, to the northwest of Cádiz, Sanlúcar is a popular get-away for families from Seville. The town is also famed for vineyards that produce the grapes for *manzanilla*, a dry fino-style sherry. The sea breezes are said to supply *manzanilla*'s distinctive salty tang.

THE COSTA VERDE

Most people have an image of Spain as a land of white sun-baked villages, bullfights and swirling flamenco dancers. However, there exists a very different Spain in the northwest: Cantabria, Asturias and Galicia consti-tute a land of fishermen and farmers, where frequent and heavy rainfall makes for a verdant landscape: the Costa Verde.

Pretty Santillana del Mar

CANTABRIA

There is plenty of variety in the autonomous region of Can-tabria, where the sea and the snow-capped heights of the Picos de Europa can both be covered in a day's excursion. As well as fishing villages, ports and miles of undevel-oped wilderness, the coast of Cantabria also offers several popular summer resorts, such as **Castro Urdiales**, **Laredo** and **Comillas**.

Santander, the capital of the region, successfully combines the roles of major port and tasteful resort, and the beach suburb of **El Sardinero**, with its flower gardens and seafood bars, contributes to the city's holiday atmosphere. Overlooking the sea from the rugged peninsula is the Victorian-style **Magdalena Palace**, built for Alfonso XIII as a summer escape. The **Museo Marítimo** MMC (Tue–Sun 10am–7.30pm, Oct–Apr until 6pm; www.cantur.com) near the port is worth a visit.

Santillana del Mar ㉙, 26km (16 miles) west of Santander, is a perfectly preserved medieval village of gold-coloured stone houses, cobbled streets, farmyards and patrician mansions. Jean-Paul Sartre described it as 'the prettiest village in Spain'. At the north end of the village is the **Colegiata** (Collegiate Church), dedicated to St Juliana (Santillana is a contraction of her name) whose tomb is inside. Its Romanesque cloister is a gem. In the convent at the other end of the village, the **Museo Diocesano** specialises in carvings of saints and angels from nearby churches. **El Capricho** (www.elcaprichodegaudi.com), an extravagant palace by Gaudí in Comillas, 18km (11.2 miles) west from Santillana, is worth a look.

The impressive limestone peaks of the **Picos de Europa**, a national park just 25km (16 miles) from the coast, form part of the wall of the Cantabrian Mountains (Cordillera Cantábrica). The N621 cuts through the dramatic **Desfiladero de la Hermida** gorge along the River Deva to **Potes**, the main

---

Altamira caves

Altamira, 2km (1.5 miles) inland from Santillana, is a cave complex dating from about 12,000bc that contains some of the finest prehistoric works of art in Europe. Access to the caves is limited to prevent further damage to the murals (Fri only; raffle-type ticketing), but there is a museum (http://museodealtamira.mcu.es) containing a faithful replica and the 30,000-year-old remains of a caveman.

gateway to the eastern Picos. Here you will find fine hiking country, fantastic scenery and good bird-watching. Don't forget to taste some *queso de cabrales* – the pungent local blue cheese traditionally matured in caves.

ASTURIAS

Asturias is a wild, rugged province known for its fiercely independent people and potent cider. They say that this is the true Spain, because it was the only corner of the country that did not succumb to the Moors when they over-ran the rest of the peninsula

Galician ría

in the 8th century. A band of Christian soldiers, led by local hero Pelayo, descended from the mountains and initiated the Reconquest with a small but significant victory over the Moors at the Battle of Covadonga in 722. A modern statue of Pelayo stands in the main square of **Covadonga**, and his remains are interred in the **Santa Cueva** (Holy Cave), where he saw a vision of the Virgin Mary that inspired his victory – now a place of pilgrimage.

OVIEDO

The Asturian capital is outwardly nondescript, but the historic core of **Oviedo** ③ has some fine monuments, plus a host of friendly *sidrerías*, bars serving the local cider (*sidra*). The **cathedral** culminates in a flourish with a tall and elaborate

Gothic tower, and its Cámara Santa (Holy Chamber) is a shrine built by Alfonso II to preserve holy relics brought from Toledo after it fell to the Moors. Behind the cathedral, the **Museo Arqueológico** (www.museoarqueologicodeasturias. com) is housed in a fine old palace-convent with a gorgeous plateresque cloister. Beyond the city centre, you will find three remarkable examples of pre-Romanesque architecture. A short walk to the northeast is **San Julián de los Prados**. On the wooded slopes 3km (2 miles) northwest of Oviedo, is **Santa María del Naranco**. The greatest of the Asturian churches, it was designed as the main reception hall of a palace built for Ramiro I in 842. Up the hill, part of the former palace chapel, **San Miguel de Lillo**, has beautiful Byzantine-style carvings.

GALICIA

Galicia is an autonomous region in the northwestern corner of the Iberian Peninsula, with its own language, *Gallego*. It is made up of the four provinces of A Coruña, Lugo, Ourense and Pontevedra. Rugged and isolated, its coastline is characterised by narrow, rocky *rías* (sea inlets) battered by the Atlantic. Galicia's scalloped coastline is perfect for boating, fishing and, when the sun does shine, swimming. Although the Atlantic coast south from La Coruña has the more spectacular *rías*, the northern indentations, the **Rías Altas**, have unspoiled resort towns and quiet beaches. The medieval village of **Pontedeume** is an old-fashioned resort with a long sandy beach. **Ortigueira** is noted for its fine beach, lush hills and folk festival. **El Barqueiro**, a picturesque fishing village, has a sandy beach, and **Viveiro**'s monuments offer a contrast to the fishing port and resort ambience. Popular with bathers and fishermen, **Foz** has a mild microclimate.

LA CORUÑA

The capital of the region and one of Spain's largest ports, **La Coruña** (A Coruña in Galician) is worth a visit for its historic old town and unusual beach. It possesses Spain's oldest lighthouse, the **Torre de Hércules**, said to be the only Roman lighthouse still in operation. The Spanish Armada sailed for England, and to defeat, from La Coruña's port in 1588. Behind the port, **Avenida de la Marina** curves east to the old town and its *galeriás* (glassed-in terraces) and historic churches and monasteries. The 16th-century **Castillo de San Antón**, guarding the harbour approaches, houses an archaeological museum.

SANTIAGO DE COMPOSTELA

Santiago de Compostela ㉛ is the third holiest shrine in Christendom (after Jerusalem and Rome). Its claim to fame

Santiago de Compostela Cathedral

originates from 813, when brilliant stars attracted a peasant to a field where the tomb of the Apostle St James (Santiago in Spanish) was revealed to him. Since then pilgrims from all over Europe have travelled the **Camino de Santiago** (Pilgrim Way) across northern Spain to this remote corner of the country, at one time the western boundary of the known world. In 1189 Alexander III decreed it a Holy City – a status shared only by Rome and Jerusalem. It is also a lively and attractive place with beautiful buildings, colourful plazas, and a largely pedestrian heart, ideal for sightseeing and relaxing. Wherever you wander in Santiago de Compostela, you will be within sight of a historic church or monastery. There are also plenty of bars and restaurants serving delicious local seafood, especially *pulpo* (octopus) fresh from the *rías* (inlets).

THE LEGEND OF ST JAMES

Unsubstantiated by the Bible, the legend of St James sprang up in the 9th century when a star is supposed to have directed some Galician shepherds to the Apostle's grave. The story goes that St James brought Christianity to Spain after the death of Christ. When he returned to Judaea, he was martyred by Herod, and his disciples fled with the body in a magical vessel with no sails or crew. It ferried them to the village of Padrón, and the body was buried nearby.

Its 'discovery' in the 9th century was hailed as a miracle, and there were several more to follow, including a ghostly sighting of St James on horseback slaying Moors by the thousand at the Battle of Clavijo in 844. These exploits earned him the title 'Matamoros' or Moor Slayer. It also elevated him to the position of patron saint of the Reconquest, and of Spain. The cult of St James spread far and wide, and by the end of the 11th century, the Pilgrim Way (Camino de Santiago) was attracting pilgrims from all over Europe.

Construction of the huge and magnificent **cathedral** (summer daily 7am–8.30pm, museum from 9am; free entry to the cathedral; www.catedral desantiago.es), replacing an earlier one built on the site where James's remains were found, began in 1075 and was completed in 1128. Numerous additions and changes have taken place over the centuries, and in the 18th century the beautifully symmetrical double staircase and towers of the Obradoiro facade were added.

Stone cross in Pontevedra's main square

Just inside the main entrance, the 800-year-old **Pórtico de la Gloria** (Door of Glory) is a marvel of Romanesque sculpture by the artist known simply as Master Mateo. A 13th-century polychrome **statue of St James** takes the spotlight on the main altar, which stands above the crypt where the saint's remains lie at rest. It's also impossible to miss the giant incense burner, the **botafumeiro**, so large that it takes several men to swing it, pendulum fashion, during ceremonial occasions.

Outside the cathedral on Plaza del Obradoiro, the **Hostal dos Reis Católicos** has a stupendous facade. Founded by Fernando and Isabel in 1499, as a pilgrim hostel, this is now a luxurious *parador* (see page 183). For an added insight into local customs, crafts and folklore, visit the **Museo do Pobo Galego** (Tue–Sat 10.20am–2pm and 4–7.30pm, Sun 11am–2pm; www.museodopobo.gal), housed in the old convent of **Santo Domingo**, which has triple helicoidal (spiral) staircases, without any supports, connecting all levels of the convent.

PONTEVEDRA

A strategic port since the Middle Ages, this is one of Galicia's most charming towns. The city's pride and joy is the plateresque **Iglesia de Santa María la Mayor** in the old fishermen's quarter. Its sculpted facade is divided into compartments, each telling a New Testament story.

The patron saint of Pontevedra, the Pilgrim Virgin, is commemorated in the curvaceous 18th-century **Iglesia de la Virgen de la Peregrina**. Nearby, the **Iglesia de San Francisco** was founded in the 14th century. The impressive provincial museum, housed in interconnecting historic mansions overlooking Plaza de la Leña, offers sections on archaeology and art, plus some exhibits on the Galician seafaring way of life.

BAYONA (BAIONA)

Bayona was the first town in Spain to learn, on 1 March 1493, of Columbus's landing in the New World (there is a replica of his ship *La Pinta* in the port). Today the town is an attractive resort, although its beaches are small and tend to become crowded in season. A few miles out of the town lies the better and wider beach of **Playa de América**. Bayona's delightful fishing port is full of traditional houses and *tapas* bars. Set on a *ría*, the town overlooks a wooded promontory where an ancient castle has been transformed into a *parador*, with wonderful views.

THE BASQUE COUNTRY

The Spanish Basque Country, or País Vasco (or Euskadi to the Basques), is an autonomous region consisting of the three provinces of Alava, Guipúzoca and Vizcaya. Along with their cousins north of the border in France, around a quarter of the Basque people speak Euskara, a language unrelated to any Indo-European family and comprising six main

Colourful dwellings in the Basque Country

dialects, with the standardised Batua ('unified' in Basque) the most widely used form. The Basques are fiercely independent of spirit and mind – so much so that the ongoing campaign for independence by the terrorist organisation ETA has cost many lives over the years. On the other hand, this pretty and normally peaceful region, with many attractive towns, is considered by many people to have the finest cuisine in Spain.

VITORIA

Vitoria (Gasteiz), the capital of Alava province and region, was founded by Sancho the Wise, the Navarrese king, in 1181. In 1200 the town passed into the hands of Castile, later growing rich on the wool trade. The medieval town centre, laid out in a concentric pattern on the fortified hilltop, is home to the 14th-century **Catedral de Santa María**. Nearby, the **Museo Provincial de Arqueología** features Iron-Age and Roman relics. The prosperous merchants built gracious Renaissance mansions and fine churches such as **San Miguel** on **Plaza de la Virgen Blanca** to the south. A monument here commemorates the Duke of Wellington's 1813 victory in the Wars of Independence. The city's spacious main square, **Plaza de España**, is a classic 18th-century Spanish ensemble, with the town hall on the north side.

SAN SEBASTIÁN

San Sebastián (Donostia), the capital of Guipúzoca province, is a beautiful city situated around the Bahía de la Concha – a semicircle of sandy beaches flanked by two

Bahía de la Concha, San Sebastián

peninsulas. Formerly a fishing and trading port, San Sebastián was elevated to the heights of favoured royal seaside resort in the mid-19th century. Having been mostly burnt to the ground on 13 August 1813 during the Wars of Independence, it has little by way of historical monuments, but it does have numerous belle-époque villas and buildings. A century later, another conflict, World War I, brought substantial changes to the city as Spain's position of neutrality and San Sebastián's proximity to France made it a convenient haven for many wealthy people endeavouring to avoid the war. This influx transformed San Sebastián, and even now it has a much more well-healed ambiance than many Spanish towns.

Pintxos are the Basque version of tapas

The **Playa de la Concha** dominates the city and makes it a popular family resort. At one end, directly under **Monte Urgull**, are the colourful streets of the **Parte Vieja** (Old Quarter), radiating from the arcaded Plaza de la Constitución. The atmosphere still recalls something of an old-time fishing village, and the narrow streets are the focus for the early evening walkabout, when locals and visitors cram the multitude of bars and restaurants. The city's oldest church, **San Vicente**, is to be found in this area, as is the **Museo de Sociedad Vasca y Ciudadanía** (www.santelmomuseoa.com), better known by its former name **Museo San Telmo**, which displays the municipal art collections and has sections on Basque history, society and crafts. Not far from the fishing port, from where there are summer-season boat trips to the **Isla de Santa Clara** in the bay, the church of **Santa María** has an ornate baroque facade. To learn more about local seafaring traditions, including whaling, take a look around the aquarium at the end of the harbour.

In nearby Getaria is the **Cristóbal Balenciaga Museo** (July–Aug daily 10am–7pm, June, Sept closed Mon; http://cristobalbalenciagamuseoa.com), dedicated to the famous Spanish designer.

BILBAO

Bilbao ❷ is the capital of Vizcaya province and was once the industrial heartland of the Basque Country. It has reinvented itself and has a thriving central district with broad boulevards and leafy parks, a metro system designed by Norman Foster, and the historic **Casco Viejo** (Old Quarter).

Until the 1990s the city had no real attractions to offer, but things changed in 1997 when the **Museo Guggenheim** (Tue–Sun 10am–8pm; www.guggenheim-bilbao.es), designed by California-based architect Frank Gehry, was inaugurated. This massive, futuristic structure, funded primarily by the Basque government, has become the symbol of Bilbao, its shimmering titanium roof rising dramatically beside the banks of the Nervión. Inside, 19 spacious galleries on three floors accommodate works predominantly from 1960 to the present day, including works from the Guggenheim collections of New York and Venice.

Bilbao's Museo Guggenheim

In addition, the **Museo de Bellas Artes** (Fine Arts Museum; www.museobilbao.com) offers a rich array of Spanish classics – El Greco, Goya, and an honest 'warts and all' portrait of Felipe IV by Velázquez – as well as Flemish and Italian masterpieces. The museum's upper floor is devoted to Basque and international 20th-century art.

CASTILLA Y LEÓN

This huge area north and west of Madrid is bordered by Portugal and the Cantabrian mountains behind the Costa Verde. An autonomous region with its capital at León, it consists of nine provinces: Ávila, Burgos, León, Palencia, Salamanca, Segovia, Soria, Valladolid and Zamora (Ávila and Segovia are covered in the Around Madrid section – see pages 38 and 42).

BURGOS

Founded in 884 as a stronghold against the Moors, **Burgos** ㉝ succumbed to the invaders but was reconquered in 951 and became the capital of Castile, an honour that it held until 1492, when the Catholic Monarchs transferred their court to Valladolid. In 1812, during the War of Independence, Burgos, then a French garrison, was besieged by Wellington's troops. It was also prominent during the Spanish Civil War, when Franco was declared Head of State there in 1936. The city subsequently became the seat of the provisional government, and it was from La Isla Palace in Burgos, on 1 April 1939, that Franco proclaimed the ceasefire.

The city's most famous citizen, born in 1026, was Rodrigo Díaz, the soldier of fortune better known as El Cid (see page 21), and his remains are interred in the **cathedral** (www.catedraldeburgos.es), which is the third largest in Spain (after Seville and Toledo). This stunningly intricate Gothic jewel is also one of the most beautiful churches in the country. Construction began in 1221 but it took 400 years to complete, and it holds attractions that are classical, historical and even eccentric. Don't miss the splendid **Constable's chapel** behind the altar, the burial place of Hernández de Velasco, Constable of Castile during the reign of the Catholic Monarchs. Gil de Siloé's altar of St Anne is partnered by his son Diego's exquisite golden stairway, built in 1519; it now leads nowhere and is only used during the highly ceremonious Easter celebrations. Look out, also, for the **Papamoscas** (Flycatcher), a clown dating from the 15th century, who sits above a clock high to the left of the main door, and opens and closes his mouth at each stroke of the bell.

Equestrian statue of El Cid

Follow the banks of the River Arlanzón, passing the decorative, crenellated **Arco de Santa María**, once the main entrance to the city. At the end of the Paseo, **El Cid** greets you, in the form of an impressive equestrian statue. Nearby is the intricate and strange facade of the **Casa del Cordón** where, on 23 April 1497, Fernando and Isabel welcomed Columbus back from his second voyage to the New World. Back across the river, two noble Renaissance houses serve as the **Burgos Museum**.

On the western outskirts of Burgos, the **Convento de las**

Huelgas was founded in the 12th century by Alfonso III. Behind fortress-like walls, the complex is something of an architectural hybrid, with Romanesque elements and an exquisite Mudéjar-Gothic cloister. Kings were crowned and buried here, and a small museum displays a collection of medieval attire. Inaugurated in 2010

Arco de Santa María, Burgos

and designed by Juan Navarro Baldeweg, the **Museo de la Evolución Humana MEH** (Museum of Human Evolution; www.museoevolucionhumana.com; Tue–Sun 10am–2.30pm, 4.30–8pm; no break in summer; free Wed pm) explains human evolution through archaeological finds from the Atapuerca Mountains.

LEÓN

León ❸❹ was founded in AD68 by the Roman 7th Legion, who built their fortifications on the hill where the cathedral now stands. During the 4th century the Romans were forced out by the Visigoths who, in turn, were defeated by the Moors early in the 8th century. By the 10th century it had been repopulated by Mozarabs (Christian refugees from the south) and, as the seat of the Kingdom of León, was considered the most important Christian city in Spain. However, in 996 the Moors invaded again and it wasn't until the 11th century that the city was finally reconquered. During the 12th century its prominence began to diminish until, in 1235, it amalgamated with Castile. Today, León is a prosperous, modern city but retains a somewhat old-fashioned ambiance.

Elaborate carved portals front León's cathedral

León's most impressive monument is the 13th-century **Catedral de Santa María de Regla** (May–Sept Mon–Fri 9.30am–1.30pm, 4–8pm, Sat 9.30am–noon, 2–6pm, Sun 9.30am–11pm, 2–8pm, Oct–Apr until 7pm; www.catedraldeleon.org). Inspired by the Gothic cathedral at Chartres in France, it has the most glorious complement of stained glass in Spain – 125 huge windows and 57 smaller glassed areas dating from the 13th to the 20th centuries. The west facade sports mismatched towers and elaborately carved portals. Tours of the cloister, an elegant mix of Gothic and Renaissance elements, lead to the **Diocesan Museum**, with archaeological exhibits and both fine and applied arts.

A few streets west of the cathedral, an equestrian statue of St Isidoro crowns the south side of the **Real Colegiata de San Isidoro** (Collegiate Church). In the Moorish invasions, the saint's relics were evacuated to León from Seville, where he had been archbishop, and they attract pilgrims to this day. The **San Isidoro Museum** (guided visits: daily 10am–2pm and 4–7pm, closed Sun pm, July–Aug Mon–Sat 9am–9pm, Sun 9am–3pm; www.museosanisidorodeleon.com) contains the **Panteón Real**, the burial place of 23 kings and queens and nine *infantas*. It also has magnificent frescoes in the 'Capilla

Sixtina' ('the Sistine Chapel of Romanesque'), and a **Chapter Treasury Room**, where notable exhibits include chalices from the early Middle Ages.

Built in 1168 for the Knights of Santiago, and later used as a pilgrims' hospice, the former **Monasterio de San Marcos** was rebuilt in the 16th century and has a magnificent plateresque facade. Today, it is one of Spain's finest *paradores*. The **Museo Arqueológico Provincial** is based in the cloister and sacristy of the adjacent church.

SALAMANCA

Hannibal made **Salamanca** ㉟ his westernmost possession when he conquered this city in the 3rd century BC. Later, under the name of Helmántica, its strategic location helped it to become an important city in the Roman Empire. In 1102, after periods of rule by the Visigoths and Moors, Salamanca was reconquered by the forces of Alfonso VI. In 1218, Alfonso IX founded the first university in Spain here, and it soon gained an international reputation. Between the 15th and early 18th centuries Salamanca was the main cultural centre of the Spanish Empire. It suffered badly during the War of Independence, and it was entered by Wellington in the summer of 1812, just before the Battle of Salamanca. The cultural importance of the city has been recognised by Unesco, which has declared it a World Heritage Site.

The social hub of Salamanca is the graceful **Plaza Mayor**, considered to be the most perfect plaza in Spain, begun in 1729 during the reign of Felipe V. The street-level arcades, illuminated by delightful lanterns, support three additional storeys and the most prominent buildings are the Town Hall and Royal Pavilion.

Salamanca has two connected, and very contrasting, cathedrals (both open Apr–Sept daily 10am–8pm, Oct–Mar daily 10am–6pm; charge includes museum and cloisters; http://catedralsalamanca.vocces.com). The **Catedral Vieja** (Old Cathedral) was begun in 1114, finished a century later, and is one of the most important Romanesque structures in the country. It has a remarkable, highly intricate 15th-century altar sculpted by the Italian, Nicolás Florentino. Look, too, for an altarpiece featuring a fine 12th-century statue known as the *Virgen de la Vega* and the unusual Mudéjar dome in the **Capilla de Talavera**. Construction of the **Catedral Nueva** (New Cathedral) began in 1513 as the old one was too small. Although it has Renaissance and baroque additions, it is considered to be one of the last Gothic structures built in Spain. Inside, the triple-naved cathedral has baroque choir stalls and 18 side chapels, of which the most notable is the **Capilla Dorada** (Golden Chapel), with 110 sculptures. The **Diocesan Museum** in the

Salamanca's Plaza Mayor, the quintessential Spanish plaza

old chapter house has a notable collection of paintings by Fernando Gallego, an underrated master of 15th-century Hispano-Flemish style.

Salamanca's **university**, founded in 1218, was one of the greatest centres of learning in medieval Europe. The 16th-century plateresque facade of the main building is highly intricate, and the lecture halls around the central patio illustrate centuries of architectural and decorative detail. The adjacent **Patio de las Escuelas** is surrounded by plateresque buildings.

Salamanca has many other attractions, including some interesting convents, the **Museo de Art Nouveau y Art Déco** in the beautiful **Casa Lis** (www.museocasalis.org; free Thu am), the circular Romanesque **Iglesia de San Marcos** (dating from 1178) and the very unusual **Casa de las Conchas** (House of Shells). The latter was built by a Knight of Santiago who decorated the exterior with hundreds of carved scallop-shells, the symbol of the pilgrimage to Santiago de Compostela.

AROUND SALAMANCA

La Alberca, the principal town of the pretty mountain region of the Sierra de la Peña de Francia, is Old Spain personified: narrow alleys are lined with simple whitewashed homes, their delicate wooden balconies weighed down by flowerpots. The highlight of the local calendar is the Feast of the Assumption (15 August), when the entire population turns out to celebrate in traditional costume.

You can walk all the way around the hill town of **Ciudad Rodrigo** in no time. Take the 2km (1.5-mile) path that follows the medieval defences past the old castle (now a *parador*). There are about a dozen worthy old mansions in town, most with interesting stone carvings and inviting patios. The Plaza Mayor is distinguished by the **Casa Consistoral**

(Town Hall), a 16th-century arcaded palace with a belfry. The exterior of the **cathedral** is covered with fine sculptural details, and still bears the marks of shellfire from a famous battle during the War of Independence, when the Duke of Wellington captured the town from French forces.

SORIA

The smallest provincial capital of Spain spreads along a poplar-shaded bend of the River Duero and typifies Old Castile. The small chapel of the **Ermita de la Soledad** contains a treasured 16th-century wooden statue of Christ. Across the street, the **Museo Numantino** specialises in relics found in the Roman ruins just north of town. Soria has an impressive collection of churches, all in toast-coloured stone and almost all dating from the 12th century. They include: **Santo Domingo**, with its Romanesque facade; **San Juan de Rabanera**, with Byzantine touches and a hint of early Gothic, and the **Co-catedral de San Pedro**, with a plat eresque portal and a Romanesque cloister. On the left bank of the river, **San Juan de Duero** used to be a monastery of the Knights Templar.

VALLADOLID

Valladolid ㊱ may be less beautiful than other cities in the region, but it has more than its fair share of history and attractions. It was the home and birthplace of Castilian kings between the 12th and 17th centuries – including Felipe II and Felipe IV; capital of the empire during the reigns of Felipe II and Felipe III; the place where Fernando wed Isabel in 1469, thus marrying the kingdoms of Aragón, Catalunya, Naples, Castile and León into a united Spain; home to Cervantes and Christopher Columbus and, in 1809, headquarters for Napoleon.

Valladolid is one of the hotbeds of the Isabelline style – a form of overblown plateresque expressed in extravagant, florid ornamentation and named after Isabel of Castile. A perfect example of this style is the elaborate facade of the **Colegio de San Gregorio**, founded in the late 15th century by Fray Alonso de Burgos, Confessor to Queen Isabella. The college has housed, since 1933, the **Museo Nacional de Escultura** (National Museum of Sculpture; http://museo escultura.mcu.es), the 'Prado' of religious statuary, with works ranging from the 13th to the 18th centuries. The star here is the woodcarving genius of the Spanish Renaissance, Alonso Berruguete, said to have studied under Michelangelo.

The focal point for the city is the massive **statue of Christ** that stands tall on its pinnacle atop the cathedral. Commissioned by Felipe II in the late 16th century, the cathedral was designed and started by Juan de Herrera,

Semana Santa parade in Valladolid

co-creator of Felipe II's Escorial complex, but completed much later, which accounts for its stylistic complexity. Inside, the highlight is the altarpiece by Juan de Juni, an Italian-trained Frenchman of the mid-16th century. One of Juan de Arfe's monstrances, dating from 1587, can be seen in the museum.

On 19 May 1506 Christopher Columbus, by then a broken man, died in the arcaded two-storey building that is now the **Casa-Museo de Colón**. It displays relics and documents relating to the Age of Discovery. The **Casa de Cervantes** commemorates Miguel Cervantes, creator of *Don Quixote*, who lived here for several years. The **Oriental Museum**, adjoining the massive edifice of the 18th-century **Royal College of the Augustinian Fathers**, has one of the best collections of its kind in Spain.

ZAMORA

A strategic walled stronghold above the right bank of the River Duero, the often besieged city of Zamora changed hands many times in the centuries of the Reconquest. To get the finest view of this appealing historic city, cross the Duero by the 14th-century bridge. From the south bank, you can

CASTLES OF CASTILLA

In Castilla it is only natural to expect to see castles, and two of the best examples are within easy reach of Valladolid. **Coca Castle**, 63km (39 miles) south of the city is a late 15th-century masterpiece of Spanish Mudéjar military design, strongly influenced by Islamic architecture. And **Peñafiel Castle**, 35km (22 miles) east of Valladolid is more than 200m (656ft) long but less than 25m (80ft) across, and sits stranded high on a lonely hilltop.

Coca Castle, a masterpiece of military design

admire the Byzantine cupola of the **cathedral**, built in the 12th century and roofed in curved stone tiles laid like fish scales. Its interior features a fine altarpiece by Fernando Gallego.

East of Zamora, the medieval hilltop town of **Toro** is a national monument. Besides splendid Romanesque churches, convents and mansions, and a ruined 10th-century castle, Toro's greatest pride is the **Iglesia Colegiata de Santa María la Mayor** (Collegiate Church of St Mary the Great). A Romanesque classic, it houses a most unusual 16th-century painting entitled *The Virgin and the Fly*, which is widely considered to be a faithful portrait of Isabel of Castile.

NAVARRA AND LA RIOJA

PAMPLONA

Moving from west to east, the Pyrenees gain altitude, and the Basque character of the countryside and the people recedes. Navarra once extended into France, but the mountains

Pamplona's 'running of the bulls' in full swing

now form a natural border between France and Spain. In fact, it is not a region that is much frequented by visitors, except at one time of the year, when they flock to **Pamplona** ③⑦ (Iruña) for the world-famous Fiesta de San Fermín (Festival of St Fermin), immortalised by Ernest Hemingway, which begins on 7 July every year.

At this time the city is swamped by tens of thousands of people in festive mood. The early morning *encierros* (running of the bulls) that are a prelude to the afternoon *corridas* (bullfights) are famous, but, in fact, this fiesta has many other planned surprises, including a huge fireworks display every night.

Visiting Pamplona at any other time of the year, you should see the **cathedral**, with its magnificent cloister, and explore the narrow and colourful streets of the former Jewish quarter, south and west of the café-lined **Plaza del Castillo**.

LOGROÑO

Logroño in La Rioja is the lively capital of Spain's premier wine region. Among medieval pilgrim travellers, the province of La Rioja was renowned for cheerful and attentive hospitality. Their first stop would have been **Santa María de Palacio**, dating from the 11th century and topped by a tall, graceful, pyramidal tower. The considerably younger **cathedral** features a generously sculpted main portal.

Behind the cathedral lie the atmospheric narrow streets of the old town.

ARAGÓN

The modern, autonomous community of Aragón is approximately coextensive with the historic Kingdom of Aragón, and encompasses the three provinces of Huesca, Zaragoza and Teruel, extending south from the Pyrenees.

HUESCA

The rugged northern section of this province is a sparsely populated and visually striking region that really is 'undiscovered' Spain. The tallest peaks of all the Pyrenees belong to Aragón, and there are several good ski resorts in Astún, Candanchú and Formigal.

THE RUNNING OF THE BULLS

Pamplona's Fiesta de San Fermín (Festival of St Fermin), specifically the *encierros* or 'running of the bulls', so entranced the writer Ernest Hemingway that he immortalised it in his novel *The Sun* Also Rises (1926). Since then, the fiesta has become an international crowd-puller, and the *encierros* are just part of the celebrations, which run the gamut from wood-chopping contests to fireworks.

The *encierros* take place daily from 7 to 12 July. At 8am when the bulls are released, serious *corredores* (runners), usually dressed in white with red sashes, attempt to run, for a few steps at least, side-by-side with the bulls along the route to the Plaza de Toros (bullring), while the main crowd are just happy to watch the bulls from behind barriers. Exciting it may be, but participants are regularly maimed and killed. Hemingway, known locally as Don Ernesto, is commemorated by a bust that stands just outside the bullring.

Jaca, the gateway to the Aragón Pyrenees and an old stop on the Pilgrim Way, has been of great military significance for at least 12 centuries, ever since it figured in one of the earliest victories over the Moors. The enormous, low-lying 16th-century **fortress** at the edge of town is a symbol of its former strategic importance. Its other notable monument is the 11th-century **cathedral**, one of the oldest in Spain. Among the highlights are the fine Romanesque frescoes, Renaissance sculptures and a plateresque altarpiece.

Parque Nacional de Ordesa, reckoned to be one of Europe's best-kept secrets, is a spectacular mountain park accessible from the village of **Torla** 60km (37 miles) northeast of Jaca. Pyrenean chamois perch on the cliffs here, as do roe deer, wild boar, and the last surviving herd of ibex (mountain goats with backward curving horns) in the Pyrenees. In the Ordesa Valley dramatic canyon walls, 1,000m (3,250ft) in height, are cloaked in ancient beech, silver fir and mountain pine forests. In summer the park can be busy, but snow prevents access from October to April.

Ordesa National Park

ZARAGOZA

Capital of Aragón and the region's one big city, **Zaragoza** ❸ can trace its origins back to the Iberians.

In 19BC the Romans founded the city of Caesaraugusta. Subsequently, the Moors held the city for 400 years until Alfonso I (The Fighter) reconquered it in 1118.

Nuestra Señora del Pilar, Zaragoza

The long, narrow **Plaza del Pilar** is the social centre of Zaragoza, and is home to magnificent monuments and modern fountains. Of the monuments, the cathedral-basilica of **Nuestra Señora del Pilar** (Our Lady of the Pillar), the largest and most important, is located in the centre. According to tradition, the Virgin Mary appeared here in AD40, standing on the jasper column that forms part of the elaborate **Capilla del Pilar**. The cathedral's superb main altarpiece is the work of the sculptor Damián Forment. Zaragoza's other cathedral, **La Seo**, was built in the 12th century. Although the cathedral is mainly Gothic, it features Romanesque remnants, Mudéjar decorations and striking baroque postscripts, plus a 17th-century belfry displaying one of the finest tapestry collections in Spain. The **Museo del Foro de Caesaraugusta** (Tue–Sat 10am–2pm, 5–9pm, Sun 10am–2.30pm) allows visitors to see the remains of the city's 1st-century Roman forum.

Between the two cathedrals is **La Lonja**, considered the finest example of civil architecture in Zaragoza and constructed as an exchange between 1541 and 1551.

To the west of the city centre, the restored Moorish **Aljafería Palace** was founded in the 11th century, then adapted by the

Teruel cathedral's 13th-century Mudéjar tower

Christian kings of Aragón after the Reconquest. Across the moat (now a sunken garden) you enter the world of Muslim Spain. Part of the palace now serves as Aragón's parliament.

TERUEL

The capital of Lower Aragón, **Teruel** is a prime showcase for Mudéjar-style architecture. When Alfonso II of Aragón captured the town from the Moors in 1171, most Muslims chose to stay until their enforced expulsion at the end of the 15th century. This was time enough for the creation of lasting works of Mudéjar art. The **cathedral's** Mudéjar elements include the finely decorated 13th-century brick tower and the lantern in the dome. Two other local towers are considered to be classics of the style: the **Torre San Martín** and **Torre del Salvador**. The Gothic **Iglesia de San Pedro** has a 13th-century Mudéjar tower. Adjoining the church is a chapel containing the mausoleum of the **Lovers of Teruel**, a star-crossed 13th-century couple whose tale of love lost and early death has inspired generations of Spanish writers.

CASTILLA-LA MANCHA

This is a geographically diverse area that wraps around Madrid to the east and south and consists of the provinces of Albacete, Ciudad Real, Cuenca, Guadalajara and Toledo (the latter is covered in Around Madrid – see page 35).

LA MANCHA

The vast, parched plain of La Mancha, with its endless, shimmering horizons, was the perfect setting for the adventures of author Miguel Cervantes' myopic, idealistic knight, Don Quixote, and his squire, Sancho Panza. The names of several of La Mancha's villages and towns appear in the text of *Don Quixote de la Mancha*, none more important than **El Toboso** (in Toledo province), the home of Dulcinea, the woman of Quixote's dreams. Dulcinea's house is open to the public.

MIGUEL DE CERVANTES SAAVEDRA

Cervantes was born on the very edge of La Mancha, at **Alcalá de Henares**, in 1547. The son of an itinerant doctor, his education was minimal. He travelled, became a soldier and was wounded in the naval Battle of Lepanto in 1571. Four years later he was captured by corsairs and held in Algiers for five years before being ransomed. It is said he wrote the first draft of *Don Quixote* in prison at **Argamasilla de Alba** (northwest of Almagro). It was published in 1605 to great acclaim, and has been translated into more languages than any other book except the Bible. A second part appeared in 1615, a year before his death.

CUENCA

Cuenca ㊴, away from the main highways in the foothills of the Sistema Iberico range in eastern Castilla-La Mancha, is not to be missed. The old town occupies a dramatic site perched on a precipice above the rivers Huécar and Júcar. It is here that Cuenca's famous medieval **Casas Colgadas** (Hanging Houses) literally hang out over the void.

The **Museo de Arte Abstracto Español** (www.march.es), housed within the Casas Colgadas, has a collection of outstanding contemporary Spanish paintings and sculptures, while the nearby **Museo de Cuenca**, a provincial archaeological museum, occupies a 14th-century palace, La Casa del Curato. The **cathedral** is a unique 12th-century Gothic/Anglo-Norman structure that underwent significant renovations in the 17th century. Its interior is very plain but the treasures here include a 14th-century Byzantine diptych embellished with precious stones, unique in Spain.

SIGÜENZA

Sigüenza, northwest of the unexciting capital, Guadalajara, is home to a classic fortress and an outsized **Plaza Mayor**, one of the most beautiful main squares in Spain. Founded by Visigoths and occupied by Moors, Sigüenza's fort was reconquered by Christian forces early in the 12th century. It became the headquarters of the bishops of Sigüenza, housing around 1,000 soldiers and more than 300 horses during the 15th century. Today, it is a *parador*. At first sight, the crenellated **cathedral** also resembles a fortress. It contains a famous sculpture, the **sepulchre of 'El Doncel'** ('The Page'). Commissioned by Queen Isabel, it honours a young servant killed fighting in Granada in 1486. Opposite, the **Museo Diocesano de Arte** packs its 14 halls with everything from prehistoric axes to an ethereal rendering of the Virgin by Zurbarán.

Hillside houses of Cuenca

EXTREMADURA

Southwest of Madrid, this undervisited region is bordered to the west by Portugal and consists of the two provinces of Cáceres and Badajoz. Extremadura reached a brief zenith during Roman times, when a provincial capital was established at Mérida, but its real fame comes from being the 'Cradle of the Conquistadores' – adventurers such as Hernando Pizarro and Diego García, who colonised the Americas in the 16th century and brought back great riches to Spain.

CÁCERES

Cáceres was founded in 34bc by the Romans, who named it Norba Caesarina. Having declined after the Romans left, the Moorish invaders brought new prosperity during their almost 400-year reign, calling it Hizn Quazri. Cáceres was finally reconquered by King Alfonso IX of León in 1229 and repopulated by families from León, Asturias and Galicia who would later become the nobility of the region. The Order of

Statue of Francisco Pizarro in Trujillo

Santiago, a brotherhood of knights, was founded here in the late 11th century, but it was not until the 16th century that the beautiful palaces and houses that give Cáceres its unique character were constructed.

From the **Plaza Mayor** you can pass through the **Arco de la Estrella** (Star Arch) into the **Old Town** and wander down a warren of streets lined with imposing buildings, sporting ostentatious heraldic shields and often topped by huge storks' nests. The **Casa de las Veletas** (Weathervane House) has been turned into a **provincial museum** featuring archaeological finds and historical costumes. It has an old *aljibe* (Arabic reservoir) in the basement. The **Centro de Artes Visuales** (http://fundacionhelgadealvear.es) features some 2,500 national and international contemporary artworks from the collection of Helga de Alvear.

TRUJILLO

The hilltop skyline of **Trujillo** ⓸ includes a heavily fortified **castillo**, which dominates the surrounding countryside, and the town is a worthy monument to its conquistador patrons. At the southwestern corner of the eccentrically shaped **Plaza Mayor** stands the **Palacio del Marqués de la Conquista**, which was built by local son Hernando Pizarro. An equestrian statue of his half-brother, Francisco, with whom he conquered Peru, stands on the square.

There are half a dozen other palaces in the town, decorated with heroic portals, historic escutcheons and pretty patios. Storks' nests crown the tower over the Gothic church of **San Martín**, whose dark nave is paved with ancient tombstones. The Romanesque and Gothic church of **Santa María la Mayor** boasts a fine *retablo* in Hispano-Flemish style. Two imposing stone seats on the balcony were built for the Catholic Monarchs, Fernando and Isabel.

GUADALUPE

The turrets, spires and crenellations of the rambling **Monasterio de Nuestra Señora de Guadalupe** (www. monasterioguadalupe.com) dominate the town from near and far. The monastery is Spain's fourth most important pilgrimage site, and guardian of a precious wooden statue of the Virgin of Guadalupe, patron saint of the conquistadors. Founded in the 14th century, and enlarged four centuries later, the monastery is an architectural hybrid, with

SONS OF TRUJILLO

Of all the conquistador towns, none is more proud of its sons' exploits than Trujillo. The most famous were the Pizarros, who conquered Peru, but other natives were Diego García and Francisco de las Casas, who founded towns called Trujillo in Venezuela and Honduras respectively, and Francisco de Orellana, the first European navigator of the Amazon.

Diego García in particular had a fearsome reputation. He was known as the Extremadura Samson and among his legendary feats of strength he is said to have picked up the font in Santa María la Mayor to carry holy water to his mother. The tombs of the Pizarros and that of García can be seen in the same church.

a flamboyant facade flanked by stern defensive towers, and with Mudéjar and Gothic cloisters. Guided tours visit the cloisters, an embroidery museum, the chapter house, and the sacristy, which houses a remarkable collection of paintings by Zurbarán and others.

BADAJOZ

The gateway to Portugal, Badajoz is the biggest city in Extremadura. The medieval walled settlement is entered through the Puerta de Palmas – an ancient fortified city gate. Another arch used to bar the way to the **citadel** overlooking the Guadiana river, where the rulers of the Moorish kingdom of Badajoz held sway. The **cathedral**, founded in the 13th century, with its heavy walls and pinnacled tower, is largely Gothic but with Renaissance additions. Inside are impressive choir stalls, paintings, tapestries and tombstones.

MÉRIDA

At the end of the Cantabrian Wars, Caesar Augustus chose to settle veteran legionnaires in the province of Lusitania. And in 25bc, Augusta Emerita was chosen to house veterans of the 5th and 10th legions. Not long after, it was designated as capital for the province and it soon grew to be the most

ALCÁNTARA – THE BRIDGE

In its day, the magnificent six-arched Roman bridge over the Tagus near Alcántara was a renowned engineering feat. No less than 194m (636ft) long, with extraordinarily high arches, it is so impressive that the town was named after it: in Arabic al-Qantara means 'the bridge'. Built entirely without mortar, the bridge has stood since its completion in ad105.

Mérida's Roman theatre

important city in the Iberian Peninsula, and one of the most important in the Roman Empire. Today **Mérida**, a modern city and capital of Extremadura, can lay claim to the greatest number of Roman remains in any Spanish town.

The highlight is the partially restored 1st-century BC **Teatro Romano**, with seating for more than 5,500 spectators where, in summer, Greek and Roman plays are staged. The elliptical **Anfiteatro** next door (also known as the Circus Maximus) was designed to hold 15,000 spectators for gladiatorial contests and chariot races. At times it was even flooded in order to host recreations of great naval battles. Almost next door is the **Museo Nacional de Arte Romano** (http://museoarteromano.mcu.es). Its beautifully displayed collections include examples of Roman statuary, locally minted coins, and paintings discovered on the podium of the arena. Around town are many other Roman monuments: a temple to Diana, an aqueduct, and a 0.8km (0.5-mile) -long bridge spanning the Guadiana.

ZAFRA

Zafra is the most attractive of southern Extremadura's towns, and is often referred to as **Seville la Chica** (Little Seville). Its charming white houses converge on two arcaded plazas – Plaza Grande and Plaza Chica – recalling its Moorish origins. The medieval **Alcázar**, now a sumptuous *parador*, was where Hernán Cortés stayed before setting off to conquer Mexico.

THE BALEARIC ISLANDS

In the western Mediterranean, the Balearics comprise a sunny cross-section of landscapes from mountainous Mallorca to the flat Formentera.

MALLORCA

For decades **Mallorca** ❹ has been Europe's playground. The island measures 72km (45 miles) by 96km (60 miles), and well over half of the population lives in the animated and cosmopolitan capital city of **Palma de Mallorca**. **La Seu**, the formidable Gothic cathedral, was founded in 1299 – after the Reconquest by Jaume I (the Conqueror) – and dominates the seafront. The interior's magnificent proportions and traditional splendour are enhanced by Gaudí's *baldachin* hanging over the main altar.

Castell de Bellver

Alongside is the island's most important building, the classical-style **Palau de l'Almudaina**, with delicately arched and covered balconies, which was once a palace for the Muslim governors. After the Reconquest, it was renovated for the medieval kings of Mallorca.

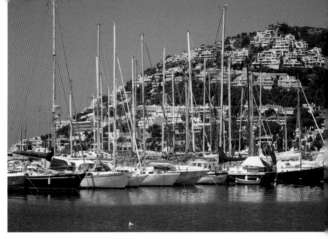

Port d'Andratx, in the west of Mallorca

High on the hill overlooking Palma and commanding both the land and sea approaches, is the distinctive cylindrical silhouette of the tower of the 14th-century **Castell de Bellver**.

Also of note are the new contemporary art museum **Es Baluard** (www.esbaluard.org), set in a former San Pere's bastion, and the collection at the **Fundación Pilar y Joan Miró** (http://miro.palmademallorca.es) where you can also visit Miro's workshop.

Exploring Mallorca's 965km (600-mile) -long coastline clockwise from Palma, the first stop must be the marina and restaurant complex of **Portals Nous**, where the size of the yachts is sure to impress. High-rise **Magaluf**, though, is attractive mainly to the Brits who flock there in tens-of-thousands. **Port d'Andratx** lies close to the western tip of the island, on a sheltered bay popular with boating fans. **Banyalbufar**, to the north, has some of the island's finest terraced orchards, and **Esporlas** has **La Granja**, a cross between a stately home, craft centre, traditional farmhouse and museum of rural life.

Attractive Deià

Valldemosa, which lies just inland, is a magnet for tourists who come to visit the monastery of **La Real Cartuja**, built on top of a royal castle. In it, you can see exhibits relating to the novelist George Sand and her companion, Frédéric Chopin, who rented rooms here between 1838 and 1839.

The next stop is **Deià**, probably the island's most attractive town, a pretty hilltop community built from honey-coloured stone. Something of an artists' colony – Robert Graves, the English poet and novelist, author of I, *Claudius*, is buried in the cemetery – this is also a good base for visiting the **Tramuntana** region in the northwest. A favourite haunt of the independent traveller, there are few beaches here, but a spectacular – and hair-raising – road allows fantastic views.

The town of **Sóller** is linked to Palma by a delightful narrow-gauge railway, with polished wood carriages making the hour-long journey through orchards and then mountain scenery. An old San Francisco-style open tram then travels the short journey down to the seaside and the pretty harbour of **Port de Sóller**.

The road between Sóller and Pollença is difficult and not particularly interesting, with the exception of the **Monestir de Lluc**, home to *La Moreneta* (the Black Madonna). **Pollença** itself is worth a visit to see the *Calvario* and a Roman bridge, while the nearby **Port de Pollença** is a very pleasant resort, not overly spoilt by tourism. To the north are the isolated and splendid cliffs of the **Cap de Formentor**. Continuing south, you will find the walled town of **Alcúdia** with its Roman ruins and popular Sunday market, and the busy beach resort of **Port d'Alcúdia**.

The main town at the easternmost end of the island is **Cala Ratjada**, a combined port and resort. **Porto Cristo**, further south, is a pleasant resort built around a protected harbour. One of the most popular tourist excursions on Mallorca, however, is a trip to the nearby **Coves del Drac** (Dragon's Caves), where you can see dramatically lit formations, and the similar **Coves de Artà**.

There are several other small towns around the lower east and southern coastlines, but none of any consequence until you arrive at **El Arenal** and the other resorts that combine to make the **Bay of Palma** the busiest area on Mallorca.

MENORCA

The second largest of the Balearic Islands, Menorca is one-fifth the area of Mallorca, and receives a much smaller number of visitors. It is a very pleasant, green and undulating island dotted with coastal towns and resorts as well as many scenic beaches and coves – some of which can only be reached on foot or by four-wheel-drive vehicle.

The capital and deep-water harbour of **Mahón** (Maó in Menorquí, the local language) was occupied by the British for a large part of the 18th century. The little city clusters on

MENORCA'S PREHISTORY

Less visited than its beaches, but nonetheless well worth closer inspection, are the numerous megalithic structures that dot the Menorcan landscape. Known by their various types as *talayots*, *taules* and *navetas*, they were built between 2000 and 800BC. During this period a civilisation developed in the western Mediterranean that has become known on the Balearic Islands as the Talayot culture.

Prehistoric taula, Torralba d'en Salord, Menorca

the cliffs above the port, and buildings in the older quarter of town have a distinctly Georgian appearance. **Ciudadela** (Ciutadella), on the west coast, also has a fine harbour, but is more akin to Andalucía than old England. **Ses Voltes**, the street leading to the Gothic cathedral that was begun in the 14th century, is all archways and completely Moorish. Visit the city museum in the **Town Hall** (Ayuntamiento) dedicated to the history of the island.

Menorca's best beach and resort is **Cala Santa Galdana**, a beautiful horseshoe-shaped cove developed in a restrained fashion. Further along the coast on the way to Maó is the **Cova d'en Xoroi**. These caves in the tall cliffs have been made into an innovative bar with fantastic views. **Fornells**, on the north coast, is another relaxed resort which also remains an active fishing port.

IBIZA (EIVISSA)

Besides those simply seeking some sun and sea, **Ibiza** ㊷ caters to the seriously hip, from assorted rock stars and artists to dance-crazy youths, and offers accommodation, restaurants, shops and entertainment accordingly.

Ibiza Town (Eivissa), the island's capital, is dominated by its old town, **Dalt Vila**, whose encircling walls are the longest in Spain. Within the walls you will find a cobbled maze packed with whitewashed houses, tiny bars, shops, flea markets and restaurants serving local fare. The capital has two archaeological museums containing a treasury of Carthaginian art. One, the **Puig des Molins**, is built adjacent to a necropolis, and tours of the burial chambers are given.

It is the beaches, though, that most people come for. They start immediately south of town, but the best, and certainly the trendiest, are generally agreed to be those at **Las Salinas. Santa Eulària**, to the north, is an important resort, as is **Sant Antoni** on the west coast, though this is very much the land of the cheap package holiday. **Portinatx** and **San Miguel**, in the north, are much smaller and quieter resorts, and you can visit caves at San Miguel.

The bright lights, loud music, exotic dress codes and, it must be said, the easy availability of drugs attract young people from all over northern Europe to Ibiza. The clubs are found mainly in the south of the island. Typical of these is **Privilege** (http://privilegeibiza.com) which, at 7,000 sq m (1.73

Enjoying Ibiza's nightlife

acres), has a capacity of 10,000 people, and advertises itself as the largest dance club in the world.

FORMENTERA

The 11km (7-mile) sea voyage from Ibiza takes 75 minutes by boat, or around half that by hydrofoil, but, whichever you choose, it's more often than not a rough passage. There is no airport here, and very little water. Once the sole retreat of the backpacker and laid-back beach bum, Formentera now caters for package tourists who come for the extensive, unspoiled beaches. There is not much to do here besides sunbathing and windsurfing.

THE CANARY ISLANDS

The seven inhabited volcanic islands that form the Canaries in the Atlantic, just off the coast of North Africa, are as different from each other as can possibly be and provide a semi-tropical escape for those in search of winter sun.

The Canaries are split into two provinces: Santa Cruz de Tenerife consists of the westernmost islands of Tenerife, little-visited El Hierro, La Gomera and La Palma; the eastern province of Las Palmas de Gran Canaria has Gran Canaria, Lanzarote and Fuerteventura. The islands appeal to differing tastes – some are better for walking, others for beach holidays.

Sons of the earth

Before the arrival of Europeans, the Canary Islands were inhabited by a people known as the Guanches, or 'sons of the earth'. Much has been discovered about their culture, including the fact that they mummified their dead and buried them in caves. Scientists place their ethnic origins in northwest Africa.

TENERIFE

The largest of the Canaries, **Tenerife** ㊸ offers more attractions and more contrasts than any of its island

Puerto de la Cruz, Tenerife

neighbours. **Santa Cruz de Tenerife**, in the northeast, is the administrative capital of the westerly Canaries. Most tourists head for the baking beaches of **Los Cristianos** and **Playa de las Américas** in the south. The island's first resort, however, was **Puerto de la Cruz** on the attractive north coast, despite having no beach. This deficiency has been overcome by the genius of the late César Manrique who designed **Lago Martiánez**, a 3-hectare (8-acre) complex of tropical lagoons and cascading fountains cleverly landscaped with lush palms and volcanic rocks to blend perfectly into the seafront. Nearby **Loro Parque** is a delight for all ages. It has the world's largest collection of parrots – more than 300 species and subspecies. It is also home to an eclectic array of animals, including gorillas, chimpanzees, tigers, jaguars, alligators, sea-lions, dolphins and numerous other creatures. The **Jardín Botánico**, founded by royal decree in 1788, is the oldest local attraction.

Orotava is the island's most picturesque town, with colonial homes and immense, traditional balconies. **La Laguna**, a World

Typical Canarian balconies

Heritage Site, preserves the impressive architecture of the early Spanish conquerors. On the north side of the island is the intriguing **Pirámides de Güimar**, where the late explorer and resident Thor Heyerdahl set out his theories about how Europeans reached the New World long ago.

The highlight of the island in every sense, **Mt Teide** is a volcanic cone in the **Parque Nacional del Teide**, and is Spain's highest mountain at 3,717m (12,200ft). In 2007 the national park was named a World Heritage Site by Unesco. Particularly beautiful in May and June when the wildflowers are in bloom, the park's spectacular scenery makes for great hiking. It is strange in mid-winter to see this gigantic snow-capped peak dominating beaches full of sun bathers. The visitor centre has details of walking trails and guided walks. You can also get to within 163m (535ft) of the summit by cable car *(teleférico)*; to avoid queues book online at www.volcanolife.com.

LA GOMERA

La Gomera remains an unspoiled island of steep, green terraced hills and tranquil valleys. Boats and hydrofoils make the short trip from Los Cristianos, arriving at **San Sebastián**. The main town, it is notable for its connections with Christopher Columbus, including a local church where he prayed and the house where he supposedly stayed in 1492. A delight for walkers, the **Garajonay National Park** is a World Heritage Site and home to the **Alto de Garajonay**, Gomera's highest peak – 1,487m (4,878ft). The island's only beach resort is in the south, at the low-key **Playa de Santiago**.

LA PALMA

The most northwesterly of the Canaries, La Palma is lush and green. **Santa Cruz de la Palma**, the capital, is an appealing small town. The main attraction here is the magnificent **Caldera de Taburiente**, a giant crater that has a circumference of some 27km (17 miles) and which drops around 700m (2,300ft) into a fertile valley. The island is perfect walking country, with marvellous views. The world-renowned Palma **observatory**, open to the public only sporadically (see www.iac.es), is on top of the **Roque de los Muchachos**, the highest peak in Palma at 2,423m (7,950ft).

GRAN CANARIA

Almost circular in shape, Gran Canaria has been described as a continent in miniature. The coastline ranges from awesome cliffs to golden dunes; inland, you can choose between stark mountains and tranquil valleys. It is also well supplied with beaches, shopping centres and sophisticated nightlife.

Teide, Spain's highest mountain

Las Palmas, capital of the island, is a major commercial centre, cosmopolitan resort and port. Its old town, **Vegueta**, with the handsome governor's residence, the 15th-century **Casa de Colón**, has well-preserved colonial architecture. The **Playa de las Canteras**, the town's sandy, restaurant-lined beach, is 3km (2 miles) long and the **Parque Santa Catalina** is one big outdoor café that buzzes night and day.

The main beach resorts are on the island's south coast. Maspalomas, or Costa Canaria, is a mega-resort made up of three parts. **Playa del Inglés** is a large, crowded package-tour centre. **Maspalomas** proper is famous for its Sahara-like dunes, which are known as an unofficial nudist beach, while **San Agustín** is quiet and tidy. West of Maspalomas, **Puerto Rico** is a family-oriented resort while **Puerto de Mogán** is an attractive fishing 'village'. **Cruz de Tejeda**, at 1,463m (4,800ft), is a popular vantage point in the rugged centre of the island, and the panorama includes two distinctive rock formations once worshipped by the Guanches.

LANZAROTE

Lanzarote is a startling place, representing the triumph of civilisation over a hostile environment. Declared a Biosphere Reserve by Unesco, the island is pock-marked with over 300 volcanoes. The locals grow onions, tomatoes, potatoes, melons and grapes, which spring in abundance from the volcanic ash. Lanzarote was the birthplace of César Manrique whose eclectic sculptures and architectural creations enhance the island. His creativity can be seen at the **Fundación César Manrique** art gallery, the prickly Jardín de Cactus, the caves of Jameos del Agua, the Monumento al Campesino and the Mirador del Río, which offers spectacular views.

Arrecife is the undistinguished capital. The island's main resort, **Puerto del Carmen**, lies to the south and has a long, golden beach, while **Costa Teguise**, just to the north of Arrecife, offers more upmarket facilities. The highlight of a trip to Lanzarote is a visit to the **Montañas de Fuego** ('Mountains of

Maspalomas dunes

Fire') in the **Timanfaya National Park**. The stark but scenically magnificent park starts just north of **Yaiza**. Its bizarre landscape of lava flows and rust-red mountains was formed over 16 months of cataclysmic volcanic activity during 1730–1. There is an information centre and car park at **Islote de Hilario**, from where bus tours depart to explore the incredible lunar landscape.

FUERTEVENTURA

Situated less than 100km (60 miles) off the coast of North Africa, and just south of Lanzarote, Fuerteventura is a bather's paradise. There are miles of golden sandy beaches, and the winds that originally blew the sand here from the Sahara still ensure superb windsurfing, for which the **Playa de Sotavento** is famous. At the southern tip of the island, the **Jandía** peninsula offers great beaches, the best of which are on **Costa Calma**. Besides watersports there is little else to do on this treeless island. **Betancuria**, the first capital, is an isolated inland oasis, and its splendid 17th-century church of **Santa María** is worth a visit.

WHAT TO DO

As well as all its historical attractions, Spain is blessed with marvellous beaches and an incredibly varied coastline. Some of Spain's resorts are very popular and crowded in the main season, but even the famous Costa del Sol still has a few relatively wild and undeveloped areas, and those seeking quieter resorts do not have to look very far to find them.

ACTIVE PURSUITS

WATERSPORTS
Fishing. For freshwater fishing, including fly fishing, especially in the Pyrenees and Cantabria, approach local tourist offices for permits. There is game fishing in the Canary Islands.

Scuba diving. There is good diving off the Costa Brava around the protected Medes islands, on the Costa de Almería, Costa Tropical and the Balearic Islands. The Canary Islands offer greater variety in deep Atlantic dives. Operators can arrange tuition, permits and equipment hire.

Water-skiing. Large resorts are fully equipped for water-skiing, jet-skiing and parasailing. The calmer waters of the Balearics and east-coast resorts at La Manga, Costa Daurada and Costa Brava are all good places to try these sports.

Windsurfing. Tuition, equipment and wetsuit hire are available almost everywhere. Advanced windsurfers chase the high winds of Tarifa in southern Spain or pick up the steady trade winds on the Jandía peninsula, Fuerteventura, and Medina, Tenerife, in the Canary Islands.

Hiking in the Picos de Europa national park

On the beach on the Costa Brava

LAND SPORTS

Golf. Spain is one of the most popular destinations in Europe for golf, and there are hundreds of top quality golf courses on the mainland and islands. Not every pro is a José María Olazábal, but the quality of instruction is generally high. The greatest concentration of courses is on the Costa del Sol, where road signs declare this also to be the Costa del Golf. On the east coast, the Valencian courses of El Saler and Escorpión are highly rated and of good value; La Manga Club on the Costa Cálida has three championship courses. On the islands, Mallorca has a number of fine courses, while Gran Canaria has Spain's oldest golf club, in a stunning setting. For an overview of what's available, request a golfing map of Spain from the national tourist office or visit www.golfspain.com.

Tennis. Many hotels and villa complexes have their own tennis courts – some even have a resident professional. The Costa del Sol is probably the biggest centre for tennis tuition and on the east coast La Manga Club is one of the best tennis centres in Europe.

Horse riding. There are ranches and equestrian centres all over the country. Many offer instruction and a range of outings on horseback, from a stimulating cross-country excursion to an overnight trek. A favourite place for this sport is the Alpujarra region, south of the Sierra Nevada.

Skiing. Most skiing resorts are in the Pyrenees (including Andorra). In the south of the country, the Sierra Nevada resort of Solynieve, just outside Granada, is also well known.

Walking, hiking and climbing. Spain has a well-marked network of long-distance footpaths denominated 'GR' (www.senderosgr. es). National, regional and local tourist offices can supply further information. Nature reserves and scenic areas have shorter hiking trails graded according to the difficulty of the terrain, from *baja* (easy) to *muy alta* (for experienced walkers only).

SHOPPING

Shops in Spain are as well equipped as elsewhere in Europe, but fans of the truly kitsch should have no fear, for among the genuinely tasteful souvenirs of a Spanish holiday – ceramics, leather goods, food treats from olive oil to nougat – the straw donkey and bullfight poster are still alive and well.

For a quick survey of what Spaniards are buying, browse through the big department stores, such as the ubiquitous El Corte Inglés. There are branches in major cities. For quality crafts, it's best to seek out the workshops of local artisans. Tourist offices will always be able to advise on their locations.

JAI-ALAI – THE WORLD'S FASTEST BALL GAME

The ancient Basque game of jai-alai (pronounced 'high-a-lie', but sometimes also known as *pelota*) is played throughout the Basque region. Every town and almost every village, no matter how tiny, has a *frontón*, or pitch, rather like a squash court, where the players hurl themselves around after the *pelota* (ball), which is propelled at the wall at speeds of up to 300kmh (188mph) by woven straw scoops attached to the players' hands.

The basic rules are similar to those for tennis or squash – the ball may only bounce once on the ground; each game comprises 7 to 9 points. Considerably more complex is the betting, which is largely incomprehensible to outsiders.

Here are a few suggestions for best buys in Spain:

Antiques. You will find few bargains in genuine antiques shops or stalls. However, some big cities have open-air *rastros* (flea markets) on Sunday mornings – those in Madrid and Sevilla are attractions in their own right – which can provide plenty of fun for browsers.

Artificial pearls. Made in Mallorca, these are so convincing that experts are often fooled. Some say the test is to rub them along your teeth – the real ones are more gritty.

Ceramics. Each region has its own distinctive designs and colour schemes. Hand-painted *azulejos* (tiles of Moorish origins) are popular and collectable. Talavera de la Reina, west of Madrid, is a major centre for top-rated ceramics. Lladró figurine collectors can stock up at stores all over Spain; less detailed models from the same factory (based in Valencia) go under the name of Nao porcelain.

Damascene and Toledo steel. This is a speciality of Toledo, although the art of damascening (inlaying the steel with intricate gold designs) originated in Damascus.

Embroidery and lace. Pretty embroidered linen and traditional lacework is sold all over Spain. Look for lace *mantillas*, lightweight shawls used for covering the shoulders, often worn over a comb in the hair. Be wary of street sellers offering bargain prices, as their goods are generally of much poorer quality and made anywhere but in Spain.

Glassware. Mallorca is a centre for glassmaking. The typical blue, green or amber bowls, glasses and jugs are sold in many mainland stores.

Leather. Top-quality Spanish leather products range from sturdy belts, wallets and riding boots to elegant handbags and jackets. Beware of the less expensive bags and belts on sale at stalls and in markets; more often than not these are imported from Morocco and you will pay two to three times the original price.

ENTERTAINMENT

Since Spaniards don't start thinking about their dinner until 9 or 10pm, Spanish nightlife tends to begin later and keep going far later than in other countries. The most popular first stop is a 'pub' or *bar de copas* – a bar playing loud music with few places to sit down. Only around 2am do people decide to move on to a club. Barcelona is one of the most fashionable nightspots in Europe. Madrid is the city that never sleeps, and Ibiza is the leader of Europe's clubbing scene.

Toledo-steel scissors

FLAMENCO

Throbbing guitars, snapping fingers, stamping heels, colourful dresses and soul-stirring songs lure local enthusiasts and visitors to Spain's flamenco nightclubs. There are two main groups of songs: the bouncier, more cheerful type is known as *cante chico*; the *cante jondo* deals with love, death and human drama in slow, piercing style. Unfortunately, most people will only get to see the show-biz style *tablaos* flamenco, for which their hotel gets a percentage for every ticket sold. For the real thing, you have to head for the specialist bars and clubs of Andalucía, home of flamenco. It's best to ask a taxi driver to take you to them as the performers often move from one location to another without much notice. In Madrid, Casa Patas (www.casapatas.com) in La Latina district is a good introduction to flamenco.

Flamenco is music to stir the depths of the soul

OTHER CULTURAL ACTIVITIES

Spaniards take opera very seriously and are proud of their home-grown stars. Among the great venues are Barcelona's Gran Teatre del Liceu (www.liceubarcelona.cat), Madrid's Teatro Real (www.teatro-real.com), Sevilla's Teatro de la Mastreanza (www.teatrodelamaestranza.es) and Valencia's Palau de les Arts (www.lesarts.com). Zarzuela theatre, a uniquely Spanish form of operetta incorporating music, dance, singing and talking, is also popular – particularly at its spiritual home of the Teatro de la Zarzuela (http://teatrodelazarzuela.mcu.es) in Madrid.

For concerts, Madrid's Auditorio Nacional de Música (www.auditorionacional.mcu.es) is home to the Spanish National Orchestra. Check with local tourist offices for details of concerts and recitals elsewhere. For drama, Spanish plays – classical and contemporary – can be seen all over the country.

Foreign films are generally dubbed before they are shown in a Spanish cinema, but in major cities and some resorts cinemas may show films in their original version (labelled 'v.o.') with Spanish subtitles.

CHILDREN'S SPAIN

Long, sunny days and soft, safe, sandy beaches mean that coastal Spain is a favourite family destination. Many hotels have special provisions for junior guests, ranging from organised

BULLFIGHTING

Like it or loathe it, it is impossible to escape the impact that the *corrida* (bullfight) has on Spanish life. The colourful *carteles* (advertising posters) are ubiquitous in Spain and the *temporada* (season) lasts from March to October. The bullfight isn't considered a sport – a contest between two equals. Instead it is a highly ritualistic event in which man pits himself against a magnificent and powerful animal. Interestingly, bullfighting has been banned from the Canary Islands and Catalonia, a move characterised as more of an act of independence towards what is quintessentially Spanish rather than motivated by animal welfare concerns.

The *corrida* consists of three *tercios* (acts), each with its own rituals. In the first *tercio*, the *toro bravo* (fighting bull) is released and the matador (literally 'killer') takes stock of the bull, making passes with his large magenta and yellow *capote* (cape). Next the *picadores* – mounted men armed with wooden poles tipped with a pointed metal head – attempt to lance the bull behind its large neck muscle, causing the bull's head to lower. In the second *tercio*, the *banderilleros*, part of the matador's team of assistants work on foot to plant long sticks with a barbed end and covered with coloured paper into the bull's back. The third and final *tercio*, the *faena*, sees the matador return, without his *montera* (hat) and armed with just the much smaller, dark red *muleta* (cape). This is what he gets paid handsomely for. For the next 13 minutes – legally it cannot last any longer, and often it is shorter – he adjusts his skills to the characteristics and strength of the bull, with intricate passes that bring man and bull into close contact. If all is going well, the band will strike up an accompanying *pasodoble*; when the matador is ready for the 'moment of truth', the most dangerous point in the *corrida*, the band will suddenly stop. It is then that the matador, *muleta* in his left hand directing the bull's attention away from his body and sword in his right, will spin over the dangerous right horn, trying to deliver an *espada* (sword) stroke between the shoulder blades and into the heart, with the aim of killing the bull instantly.

poolside games and outings to babysitting facilities. When sea-water and sandcastles start to wear thin, you can try some of the following:

Make a splash. Water parks are a highly popular alternative. While kids shoot down waterslides and ride the machine-made waves, parents can top off their tans in landscaped gardens. Additional attractions often include bowling and mini-golf.

Go-karting. A favourite with the children (not to mention their parents), go-kart tracks are common along the *costas* and in the islands.

A night out. The Spanish take their children out at night, so why not do likewise? Older children will probably enjoy a colourful flamenco show, and there are no restrictions on children accompanying adults into bars, restaurants or cafés, as long as they are well behaved.

Fiesta. Older children will love the firework displays and music, while the younger ones watch the dancers and giant papier-mâché figures. Carnival is always a colourful event, where the local children usually wear the best costumes. Larger fiestas often have special entertainment for children.

Fair rides. Most big cities or resorts have a *parque de atrac-ciones* where the rides range from the old-fashioned carou-sel and big wheel to high-tech thrills. Barcelona's funfair at Tibidabo (www.tibidabo.cat), accessible by funicular railway, deserves a special mention for its old-fashioned rides and tremendous views.

Theme parks. Spain's biggest theme parks are Port Aventura (www.portaventura.es) on the Costa Daurada, Terra Mítica (www.terramiticapark.com) near Benidorm, Isla Mágica (www.islamagica.es) in Seville, Warner Brothers Movie World (http://parquewarner.com) outside Madrid, Palmitos Park (www.palmitospark.es) on Gran Canaria and Loro Parque (www.loroparque.com) on Tenerife.

FESTIVALS

The best way to experience Spanish customs is to watch a *fiesta* (festival), held in honour of the local patron saint and offering locals the chance to dress up in costume, dance through the night, let off firecrackers or run with bulls. Every community, whatever its size, has its own *fiesta* – with the larger towns and cities often celebrating more than one. Check with the tourist office for details of local celebrations during your stay. Here's a selection of the very best from around the country:

February/March: Carnival before the beginning of Lent. Processions in Santa Cruz de Tenerife, Cádiz, Sitges and many other places.

March/April: Las Fallas Festival in Valencia, with the setting alight of hundreds of papier-mâché figures. Semana Santa (Holy Week) sees the processions of hooded penitents in all major cities from Palm Sunday until Easter Sunday, with the most famous in Sevilla.

April: Sevilla's famous Feria (Spring Fair) with colourful costume parades, plenty of *sevillana* music, and bullfights. In Alcoi and other towns on the Costa Blanca people stage mock battles between 'Moors and Christians'.

May: Festival of the Patios in Córdoba and International Horse Fair in Jerez de la Frontera.

May/June: Fiesta de San Isidro: bullfighting, concerts and funfairs in Madrid. Corpus Christi: festivities everywhere, especially in Granada, Toledo, Sitges and the Canary Islands. El Rocío pilgrimage in Andalucía.

July: Fiesta de San Fermín: bullruns, bullfights and festivities in Pamplona. Festival of the Virgen del Carmen, patroness of fishermen. Festival of St James, Santiago de Compostela, with firework displays and bonfires.

August: Assumption: national holiday on August 15 with numerous towns holding festivals.

September: Logroño Wine Harvest: wine festival in Jerez de la Frontera. Mercè Festival: music and folklore in Barcelona.

October: Fiestas del Pilar Festival: processions, bullfights and folklore in Zaragoza.

EATING OUT

The Spanish take their food very seriously and you will rarely be disappointed by the variety and flavour of the hearty portions served in local *restaurantes* throughout Spain. Each region has its own distinctive culinary strengths, from the seafood creations of the north to the rice platters of the east, from the roasts of the central area to the succulent hams and fried fish of the south. And for every dish, there is usually a locally grown wine to match.

WHERE TO EAT

Venta, *posada*, *mesón*, *casa de comidas* and *fonda* are all synonyms for 'restaurant'. Many bars also double as restaurants, serving both *tapas* and full meals. The menu will be displayed outside or at the door, giving an idea of what you can expect to pay (see page 150).

Most restaurants offer a good value *menú del día* (daily special). This is normally a three-course meal, including house wine, at a reasonable set price, although it may only be available at lunchtime on week days.

The prices on the menu include a service charge and taxes, but it is customary to leave a tip of 5 to 10 percent if you have been served efficiently. Bars and cafés, like restaurants, usually include a service charge, but additional small tips of a few coins are customary. Prices are slightly lower if you stand or sit at the bar rather than occupy a table.

Two notes of caution: the prices of *tapas*, those tasty bar snacks, are not always indicated and can be surprisingly expensive: it is not unusual for the cost of several *tapas* to equate to or exceed the price of the *menú del día*. Also, ask how much your meal will cost when ordering fish or seafood that is priced by the 100g weight. The price is based on the uncooked weight and can be more than you expected.

Meal times are generally later in Spain than in most parts of Europe. Peak hours are 2–3.30pm for lunch and 9–11pm for dinner. However, in tourist areas or big cities, you can get a meal at most places just about any time of day.

WHAT TO EAT

BREAKFAST

For Spaniards, this is the least significant meal of the day and will probably just consist of *tostada* (toast) or a roll and coffee. If you have a sweet tooth, *churros* are deep-fried sugared doughnut-like temptations, made for dipping into your coffee or a cup of hot chocolate. To make guests feel at home, most hotels offer breakfast buffets with a selection of cereals, fresh and dried fruit, cold meats and cheeses, plus bacon and eggs.

Cerveza on tap

LUNCH AND DINNER

The classic Spanish dish is *paella*, named after the black iron pan in which saffron-flavoured rice is cooked in stock. True Valencian *paella* is made with chicken and rabbit, but there is also a seafood variety and many restaurants serve a 'mixed' variety, which can have all sorts of ingredients. It is always cooked to order (usually for a minimum of two people) and outside of tourist areas is served only at lunch.

There are two other national favourites well known to visitors. The first is *gazpacho*, an Andalucían chilled soup made with chopped tomatoes, peppers, cucumbers, onions and fried croutons. The second is *tortilla de patata*, or potato omelette. There are many variations on this theme, served hot or cold.

REGIONAL TASTES

Every province – and almost every town – in Spain seems to have its own locally produced sausage, cheese or variation on *cocido*, a rich cold-weather meat and vegetable hot-pot. Here are a few suggestions for what's cooking around the country, moving roughly north to south.

Galicia: Famed for seafood, notably *pulpo* (octopus); try also *caldo gallego* (a hearty vegetable soup), *empanada* (pies stuffed with meat or seafood, served hot or cold), *lacón con grelos* (boiled ham with turnip greens) and paprika-laced dishes.

TAPAS

A *tapa* is a small portion of food, usually served with a slice or two of French bread, which encourages you to keep drinking instead of heading off to a restaurant for a meal. Once upon a time, *tapas* were given away, but that is rare these days. Even so, bars that specialise in *tapas* are more popular than ever.

Good *tapas* bars have a whole counter displaying hot and cold dishes, making it easy to make a choice – just point to one you like the look of. Typical offerings are olives, meatballs, local cheese, prawns in garlic, marinated anchovies, *chorizo* (spicy sausage), and wedges of Spanish *tortilla* (omelette). *Una tapa* is the smallest amount you can order; *media ración* is half a small plateful, and *una ración* is almost a meal in itself.

Asturias: Look out for *fabada asturiana* (big white bean and sausage casserole), *merluza a la sidra* (hake in cider sauce), and *queso de Cabrales* (pungent, piquant, creamy blue cheese).

Basque country: Seafood is king here, in the form of *bacalao al pil pil* (fried cod in hot garlic sauce), *chipirones* (tiny squid), *marmitako* (spicy tuna, tomato and potato stew) and

Cured hams are a speciality of the mountainous regions

merluza con almejas y gambas (hake with clams and prawns).

The Pyrenees: Hearty, warming meat dishes are served in *chilindrón* sauce (tomatoes, peppers, garlic, ham and wine); look out for game dishes, and mountain trout.

Catalonia: This region is noted for *esqueixada* salad (grilled or baked vegetables in olive oil), grilled fish with *romesco* sauce (nuts, chilli, tomatoes, garlic and breadcrumbs), and seafood stews, such as *zarzuela* and *suquet de peix*.

Castile: Try *sopa castellana* for starters (a baked garlic soup with chunks of ham and an egg poaching in it), followed by *cochinillo asado* (suckling pig) or *cordero asado* (roast lamb).

The east coast: Valencia is the original home of *paella* and many other rice-based dishes.

La Mancha: Quixote country is famed for such game dishes as *tojunto* (rabbit stew), but also for *pisto manchego* (an extravagant ratatouille-like vegetable stew of red peppers, onions, aubergines, tomatoes and courgettes) and *manchego*, which is Spain's favourite cheese made with sheep's milk.

Extremadura: The region is noted for country-style pork and lamb and countless varieties of sausage.

Andalucía: Specialities in this region include cold soups, *gazpacho* and *ajo blanco* (or *gazpacho blanco*, made from garlic and almonds garnished with grapes), *fritura mixta* or *pescaito frito* (pieces of fish fried in a light batter) and *huevos a la flamenca* (egg, tomato and vegetable baked with *chorizo*, prawns and ham).

The Islands: Canarian specialities include *papas arrugadas* (new potatoes baked and rolled in rock salt) served with *mojo picón* (piquant red sauce) and *mojo verde* (green herb sauce served with fish). On Mallorca, sample *tumbet* (ratatouille and potato casserole with meat or fish).

SWEET-TOOTH SPECIALS

The ubiquitous Spanish dessert is the egg-based flan *(crème caramel)*. The Catalans do a deluxe version, *crema catalana*, flavoured with lemon and cinnamon. Many towns have their own recipes for *yemas*, a sweet egg-yolk and sugar confection.

Octopus is a speciality of Galicia

Otherwise, you can head for the *pastelerías* (cake shops) for a vast repertoire of cakes, tarts and pastries. *Mazapán* (marzipan) and *turrón* (nougat) also come in various guises.

WHAT TO DRINK

WINES AND ALCOHOLIC DRINKS

Spain has more square kilometres of vineyards than any other European country. Vintage pundits confidently compare the best Spanish wines with the most respected French classics, causing much controversy in some global wine circles. On the other hand, much of the crop is ordinary, intended for home consumption and never meant to grace the glasses of experts or travel far.

The better Spanish wines are regulated by the Denominación de Origen quality control. If a bottle is marked DOC, you can be sure the wine was made in a particular region and its producers followed the strictest rules.

The oldest and most vigorously protected wine *denominación* is Rioja, and some truly distinguished reds *(tinto)* are grown along the Ebro Valley in northern Spain. East of La Rioja, Aragon contributes some powerful Cariñena reds; quality reds are also produced in Ribera del Duero. The best-known wines from central Spain, the splendidly smooth reds of Valdepeñas, come from La Mancha.

The Penedés region of Catalonia is acclaimed not only for its excellent still white wines *(blanco)*, but also for its *cava*, a sparkling wine made by the *méthode champenoise*; it is a revitalising and refreshing chilled drink.

In the southwest, Jerez de la Frontera is the home of sherry. As an aperitif, try a chilled, dry *fino* or medium-dry *amontillado*. A dark, sweet *oloroso* goes down well after dinner. Spain also produces several sweet dessert wines, such as muscatel, which tastes of sultanas and honey.

A glass of fino sherry

Spanish brandy is often sweeter and heavier than French Cognac. It is sometimes an ingredient in *sangría* – a popular tourist drink – whose other ingredients are red wine, orange and lemon juice, lemonade, sugar, sliced fruit and ice.

Beer *(cerveza)* is generally of the pils, or lager, variety, and not very strong. There are plenty of Spanish brands, and foreign beers are widely available. A small draught beer is *una caña pequeña*, a medium size one is a *tubo* and a large one (not always available) – a *grande* – is about the same size as a pint. Bottled beer is sold in a one-third litre bottle – *una botella* – or a one-quarter litre bottle – *un botellín*. Bottles are more expensive than draught.

TEA, COFFEE AND SOFT DRINKS

The Spanish usually drink coffee *(café)* as opposed to tea *(té)*. This can be either *solo*, small and black, *con leche*, a large cup made with milk, or *cortado*, a small cup with a little milk. Americans may find Spanish coffee strong.

Mineral water *(agua mineral)* is either sparkling *(con gas)* or still *(sin gas)*. Ice cream parlours *(heladería)* sell *granizado*, slushy iced fruit juices, and many bars serve fresh orange juice *(zumo de naranjas naturales)*, though this can be surprisingly expensive considering oranges are one of Spain's main crops.

TO HELP YOU ORDER...

Could we have a table? **¿Nos puede dar una mesa?**

Do you have a set menu? **¿Tiene un menú del día?**

I'd like... **Quisiera...**

beer **una cerveza**	mineral water **agua mineral**
bread **pan**	
coffee **un café**	potatoes **patatas**
dessert **un postre**	rice **arroz**
fish **pescado**	salad **una ensalada**
fruit **fruta**	sandwich **un bocadillo**
glass **un vaso**	sugar **azúcar**
ice cream **un helado**	tea **un té**
meat **carne**	water (iced) **agua (fresca)**
menu **la carta**	
milk **leche**	wine **vino**

MENU READER

aceitunas olives	**langostino** large prawn
albóndigas meatballs	**lomo** loin
atún tuna	**mariscos** shellfish
anchoas anchovies	**mejillones** mussels
bacalao cod	**melocotón** peach
besugo sea bream	**merluza** hake
boquerones fresh anchovies	**navajas** razor clams
calamares squid	**ostras** oysters
cerdo pork	**pastel** cake
chuleta chops	**pollo** chicken
cocido stew	**pulpitos** baby octopus
cordero lamb	
entremeses hors-d'oeuvre	**salsa** sauce
gambas prawns	**ternera** veal
langosta spiny lobster	**tortilla** omelette
	trucha trout

PLACES TO EAT

We have used the following symbols to give an idea of the average cost of a meal for two, excluding drinks:

€€€€ over 70 euros	€€€ 50–70 euros
€€ 30–50 euros	€ under 30 euros

ÁVILA

Doña Guiomar €€€ *Tomás Luís de Victoria 3, tel: 920 253 709.* This restaurant combines traditional style with classic and modern influences to create temptingly delicious dishes.

BARCELONA

Botafumeiro €€€€ *Gran de Gràcia 81, tel: 932 184 230;* www.bota fumeiro.es. Open daily for lunch and dinner. The city's top seafood restaurant is big and informal with plenty of action. The perfectly prepared and presented fish and shellfish dishes combine the best elements of Galician and Catalan cuisines. Great *tapas*: to get a seat at the seafood bar, go during off-peak times (noon–1pm, 7–8pm).

La Fonda €–€€ *Escudellers 10, tel: 933 017 515,* www.grupandilana. com. This modern restaurant set on two levels is immensely popular, especially at lunchtimes, as the queues outside testify. It is worth the wait for very good food at very reasonable prices.

Montiel €€€€ *Flassaders 19, tel: 932 68 37 29,* www.grupmontiel.com. A long-time favourite of Barceloneses, located in the picturesque El Born District. Expect a Spanish and Mediterranean menu, carefully selected wine list and excellent service in elegant surroundings. Superb degustation menu. Open daily for lunch and dinner.

CÓRDOBA

El Churrasco €€€ *Romero 16, tel: 957 290 819,* http://elchurrasco. es. Located in a 14th-century house in the Jewish quarter, with various dining areas each uniquely decorated. The seasonal cuisine is based on natural products, with wines from its own Museo del Vino (Wine Museum). Closed August.

COSTA DEL SOL

Taberna del Alabardero Club de Playa €€€€ *Club de Playa Alabandero, Urbanización Castiglione, San Pedro de Alcantara, tel: 952 780 552,* http://grupolezama.es. A beach restaurant specialising in paellas and fried fish.

GRANADA

Sevilla €€€ *Oficios 12, tel: 958 221 223,* www.restaurantesevilla.es. Situated next to the cathedral, Granada's most famous restaurant was also once a favourite haunt of the renowned poet and dramatist Federico García Lorca. The menu offers a good mixture of local Granadino and Andalucían specialities. Closed Sunday evening.

MADRID

Casa Botín €€€ *Cuchilleros, 17, tel: 913 664 217,* www.botin.es. Believed to be the oldest restaurant in the world, having opened its doors in 1725. Adjacent to the Plaza Mayor, it specialises in suckling pig roasted in a wood-fired oven.

La Bola €€ *Bola, 5, tel: 915 476 930,* www.labola.es. A Madrid institution that has been going since 1870. The place to eat an authentic dish of *cocido madrileño*, the city's hearty trademark stew. Closed Sunday evening.

Lhardy €€€€ *San Jerónimo 8, tel: 915 222 207,* www.lhardy.com. At first glance this looks like a very elegant and old-fashioned delicatessen. Founded in 1839, that is exactly what it is downstairs, but upstairs is a suite of elegant dining rooms, where you can expect a traditional gastronomic treat, whatever you select from the menu. Closed August; June and July lunch only.

Taberna del Alabardero €€€ *Felipe V 6, tel: 915 472 577*, http://
grupolezama.es. Located close to the Royal Palace, it acquired the
name Guardia de Alabarderos tavern because it was a popular wa-
tering hole for the guards who used to march by on duty and return
later for a drink. Now a fine restaurant serving excellent Basque
food at remarkably good value – especially the *menú del día*.

PAMPLONA

Anttonenea €€€ *Calle San Anton 48, tel: 948 104 445*, www.restaurante
anttonenea.com. Enjoy a big choice of grilled meat, as well as fresh
fish dishes and salads. Good value *menu del dia* (€22) with coffee,
water and a glass of wine or beer. Closed Monday in summer.

SALAMANCA

Casa Paca €€€ *Plaza del Peso, 10, tel: 923 218 993*, www.casapaca.
com. Very close to the Plaza Mayor this restaurant, with a classical-style decor, serves hearty Castilian traditional fare such as
lentejas con chorizo (lentils with sausage), *cocido* (chick-pea stew),
alubias (white bean stew), green peppers stuffed with ox tail and
fried kid. It also does good salads and fish dishes and there is a
range of *tapas* available from the bar.

SAN SEBASTIÁN

Arzak €€€€ *Avenida Alcalde Elosegui 273, tel: 943 278 465*, www.
arzak.es. This acclaimed Michelin three-star restaurant specialises
in traditional Basque cuisine. The superbly prepared game and seafood dishes are accompanied by a selection of classic wines. Closed
Sunday evening, Monday and for two weeks in June and November.

SANTIAGO DE COMPOSTELA

A Barrola €€–€€€ *Rua Franco 29, tel: 981 577 999*, http://
restaurantebarrola.com. Passers-by are tempted in by a

sumptuous window display of fish and shellfish. The house speciality is a shellfish combination, designed to be shared by two. The octopus in garlic with mussels is equally delicious.

SEGOVIA

José María €€€ *Cronista Lecea 11, tel: 921 466 017*, www. restaurantejosemaria.com. A firm favourite in Segovia, José María serves traditional Castilian fare with fine local wines in a lively, rustic ambiance. It is hard not to over-indulge in the wide selection of tapas on show in the bar.

SEVILLE

Egaña Oriza €€€€ *San Fernando 41, tel: 954 227 211*, www. restauranteoriza.com. A renowned restaurant located in a beautiful building just across from Seville's old Tobacco Factory (the setting for Bizet's opera *Carmen*). It is famous for Jose María Egaña's dishes, which combine Basque influences with Andalucían traditions. The wine list features Spanish and international vintages. Closed Sunday in June and July, and the whole of August.

Mechela €€€€ *Calle Bailen 34, tel: 955 289 493*. Near the Museo de Bellas Artes, this has a delightful ambiance and decor and offers an amazing array of *tapas*, seafood, typical Andalusian dishes and excellent service. Booking essential. Closed Sun and Monday lunch, and the whole of August.

TOLEDO

La Orza €€€–€€€€ *Descalzos 5, tel: 925 223 011*, http:// restaurantelaorza.com. Located in the Jewish quarter near the El Greco Museum this fine restaurant spices up traditional Spanish fare and Castilian specialities, with dishes such as pork tenderloin served with Parmesan ice cream and a pine nut praline. Extensive wine list. Closed Sunday night.

VALENCIA

L'Estimat €€–€€€ *Avenida de Neptuno 16, Playa de las Arenas, tel: 963 711 018*. An institution on the Valencia beach that has been serving regional rice dishes, fresh fish and seafood since 1927. Closed Monday evening and all day Tuesday.

THE BALEARIC ISLANDS

IBIZA

Restaurante del Carmen €€ *Platja Cala D'Hort, Sant Josep de Sa Talaia, tel: 971 187 449*. What this restaurant lacks in style it more than makes up for in location. It overlooks the beach and has, arguably, the best views of the mystic Es Vedra rock.

Sueño de Estrellas €€€€ *Urbanización Na Xamena, Port de San Miguel, tel: 971 334 500*, www.hotelhacienda-ibiza.com. The gourmet restaurant of the Hotel Hacienda Na Xamena is set on two levels overlooking the pool and cliffs. Whether you select the daily menu, the special seven-course menu or à la carte, expect delightfully thought-out and well-presented dishes.

MALLORCA

3/65 €€€€ *Ctra Palma-Pollenca, km50, Port de Pollença, tel: 971 535 353 ;* http://sonbrull.com. This is the gourmet restaurant of the boutique hotel Son Brull. With the beautiful Mediterranean landscape as a backdrop, enjoy the best of classical Mallorcan cuisine. Dinner only, closed Tuesday.

El Olivo €€€€ *Son Canals, Deià, tel: 971 639 046*, www.belmond.com. One of the island's top restaurants, part of La Residencia Hotel, with terrace dining that is difficult to top for sheer romance. Delicious nouvelle cuisine. Try the gastronomic menu if you feel flush. Serves dinner only.

Ses Porxeres €€€ *Carretera Palma-Soller, Km17, Bunyola, tel: 971 613 762*. A beautiful Catalan restaurant near the Jardins d'Àlfabia.

Specialities include game, fish stews and lamb cutlets grilled on hot rocks at your table. Reservations essential, especially for Sunday lunch. Closed Sunday evening, Monday and August.

Ses Rotjes €€€–€€€€ *Carrer Rafael Blanes 21, Cala Ratjada, tel: 971 563 108*, www.sesrotges.com. This restaurant, in the hotel of the same name, has a Michelin star and is a delightful find. Although fresh fish is their speciality, they don't neglect the meat dishes. An extensive wine list. Reservations advisable. Closed Sunday.

Son Gener €€€ *Carretera Vella Son Servera – Artà Km 3, Son Servera, tel: 971 183 612*, www.songener.com. Organic restaurant near the northeastern tip of the island, and part of an exquisite boutique hotel. The vegetables and eggs are home produced and the other ingredients locally sourced.

MENORCA

Son Granot €€–€€€ *Carretera Sant Felip, Es Castell, tel: 971 355 555*, www.songranot.com. The restaurant of a lovely hotel occupying a 300-year-old red-painted house. The menu changes regularly according to market availability but always includes locally sourced seafood.

THE CANARY ISLANDS

FUERTEVENTURA

Don Antonio €€€ *La Vega del Río Palma (Betancuria), tel: 667 513 713*. One of the best restaurants on the island, serving original dishes made with locally sourced ingredients in a 17th-century country-house setting. Closed Monday.

GRAN CANARIA

La Corona de Arucas €€€ *Montaña de Arucas, tel: 649 330 287*, www.lacoronadearucas.com. A large glass-fronted restaurant on top of a hill in the north of the island (not far from Las Palmas) from which there are great views over to Mount Teide. There are a variety of options for eating, ranging from *tapas,* grilled meat, fish to salads.

LA GOMERA

Club Laurel €€€€ *Lomada de Tecina, 38810 Playa de Santiago, tel: 922 145 850,* www.jardin-tecina.com. The à la carte restaurant of the Jardín Tecina resort is located by the beach, and is reached by means of a lift that passes through the cliff. Romantic ambiance, live guitar music, haute cuisine and fine wines. Open evenings only, closed Sunday. Reservations are essential.

LA PALMA

Restaurante La Placeta €€€ *Placeta Borrero 1, Santa Cruz de la Palma, tel: 922 415 273,* www.restaurantelaplaceta.com. Located in a charming old house, this restaurant has a delightful ambiance. Wooden floors, beams, staircase and old windows are the setting for home-cooked, international-style cuisine with an emphasis on fish, meats and sauces.

LANZAROTE

Caserio de Mozaga €€€ *Malva 8, San Bartolomé, tel: 928 520 060,* www.caseriodemozaga.com. A modern restaurant, part of a charming hotel, in the stables of an old country house serving a menu strong on fish and seafood.

TENERIFE

Casa del Vino La Baranda €€€ *San Simón 49, El Sauzal, Autopista general del Norte, Km21, tel: 922 572 535;* www.casadelvinotenerife. com. This restaurant in a farmhouse built in traditional Canarian style on a 17th-century estate forms part of a wine museum. It is the perfect place for an introduction to the island's cuisine and can be found just outside El Sauzal.

A–Z TRAVEL TIPS

A Summary of Practical Information

ACCOMMODATION (see also Camping and Recommended Hotels)

Those travelling independently will find a wide range of options. For a comprehensive listing of accommodation and rates throughout Spain, consult the *Guía Oficial de Hoteles*, available from the Spanish National Tourist Office (see page 176) and larger bookshops.

By law, prices must be displayed in the reception and in the room, showing seasonal adjustments. Meals (including breakfast) are not usually included in the basic price, and VAT (IVA in Spanish) will be added to your bill.

Establishments in Spain are graded by each of the 17 autonomous governments, and may vary from region to region. More expensive hotels will have air conditioning where necessary, and rooms will have showers. Hotels are rated according to the system detailed below, with one of the following ratings plus the appropriate number of stars:

Hotel (H): rated one to five stars according to services offered.

Hotel Residencia (HR): a hotel without a restaurant, but often with a bar and cafeteria facilities.

Motel (M): rated same as hotels, but motels are few and far between in Spain.

Hotel Apartamentos (HA): apartments with hotel services and facilities, and rated the same as hotels.

Residencia Apartamentos (RA): residential apartments without a restaurant, rated the same as hotels.

Hostal (Hs): a more modest hotel, often a family concern, graded from one to three stars. Rates overlap with the lower range of hotels. A three-star *hostal* can cost about the same as a one or two-star hotel.

Hostal Residencia (HsR): a *hostal* without a restaurant.

Pensión (P): a boarding house, graded one to three stars, with only basic amenities and usually shared bathrooms.

Ciudad de Vacaciones (CV): a hotel complex complete with sports facilities.

Casa Rural: a country or village house offering bed-and-breakfast or self-catering accommodation.

Parador: a state-run hotel, often housed in a castle or other historic building, always in a fine setting and furnished in local style. Prices are mostly in line with those of a four- to five-star hotel. Advance booking is advisable. For information and bookings in Spain contact the Paradores de Turismo, Central de Reservas, Requena, 3, 28013 Madrid, tel: 902 547 979 or www.parador.es; in the UK contact Keytel International, The Foundry, 156 Blackfriars Road, London SE1 8EN, tel: 020-7953 3020; in the USA and Canada contact Marketing Ahead, 381 Park Avenue South, Suite 718, New York, NY, tel: 1 800 223-1356 or 212-686-9213, email: mahrep@ aol.com.

I'd like a single/double room. **Quisiera una habitación individual/doble.**
with bath/shower **con baño/ducha**
What is the rate per night? **¿Cuál es el precio por noche?**

AIRPORTS (see also Getting There)

Madrid's Barajas Airport (14km/9 miles northeast of the capital) is the main gateway to Spain from North America, but there are direct flights to Barcelona and Málaga. Other important international airports are Alicante, Seville and Valencia. There are also major airports on Mallorca, Tenerife and Gran Canaria.

Madrid is Spain's main air transport hub, and airlines such as Iberia and Spanair offer frequent connections to regional airports throughout the country and to the Canary Islands and the Balearics.

B

BUDGETING FOR YOUR TRIP

Accommodation. Although Spain is sometimes thought of as a budget destination, hotel prices in the cities can be comparable with other European cities, so if you are planning a city-based stay on a limited budget choose your accommodation carefully. Rates for a double room can range from as low as €50–60 at a *pensión* or *hostal* to as much as €360–420, or even more, at a top-of-the-range, 5-star hotel. As a rule of thumb, a good 4-star hotel will cost in the range of €100–150. Prices normally exclude breakfast and IVA (value added tax).

Car hire. Car hire costs are generally lower than average for Europe, but prices vary, so shop around. Fly-drive deals are often good value. If you want a small, manual-transmission car primarily for local use, it is generally cheaper to hire from a local company, especially on the Costas and the islands (see also Car Hire).

Meals and drinks. While simple meals and drinks are good value, prices vary considerably, according to where you choose to eat. The cheapest three-course meal with one drink, *menú del día*, in a small bar/restaurant will be around €12–15. Dinner in a medium-level restaurant will be about €20–30 per head, including wine. At the top restaurants expect to pay anything over €50 per person, plus wine.

Entertainment. Approximate prices are: cinema €6–8, flamenco club (entry and first drink) from €25, nightclub from €10, amusement/theme park (per day) around €25–35 adult or €17–25 child, bullfight €20–90, but prices may vary between regions.

Sightseeing. Admission prices for most museums cost, on average, €8–15. Some places have no admission charge, and there are often student discounts and other concessions, including free entry for EU citizens on certain days.

Taxis. Taxis are generally inexpensive, with a typical short city-centre ride costing around €10 on the meter. Be sure to agree the rate for long-distance journeys beforehand.

C

CAMPING

Spanish campsites are divided into categories, and rates and facilities vary accordingly. All sites, however, have drinking water, toilets and showers, electricity and basic first-aid facilities, and all are under surveillance night and day. Rates depend to a large extent on the facilities available. For a complete list of campsites, consult the *Guía de Campings*, available from the Spanish National Tourist Office (see page 176) and some local bookshops.

Camping outside of official sites is fine, provided you obtain permission from the landowner. Many campsites have good beach locations but you are not allowed to pitch your tent on tourist beaches, in urban areas, or within 1km (0.5 mile) of an official site.

CAR HIRE (see also Driving)

Hiring a car before you go avoids any uncertainties and can be cheaper too. Auto Europe (www.autoeurope.com) is one of the largest organisations offering discount rates – especially if you require a car with automatic transmission or specialist vehicles such as 4-wheel drives. Fly-drive deals with airline companies can be good value: all the big car-hire companies have discount deals with airlines. The website www.easycar.com offers inexpensive deals.

Otherwise, you'll find a choice of car-hire firms in any major town, with the market leaders – Avis, Hertz, Europcar – at the airports and principal railway stations. Rates and conditions vary

I'd like to hire a car (tomorrow). **Quisiera alquilar un coche (para mañana).**
for one day/a week **por un día/una semana**
Please include full insurance. **Haga el favor de incluir el seguro a todo riesgo.**

enormously. CDW insurance cover should be considered a necessity. Extra insurance cover against theft of radio and other car parts, and damage caused by thieves, is worth considering.

Normally you must be over 21 to hire a car, and you will need a valid driver's licence that you have held for at least 12 months, your passport and a credit card – to use to leave a deposit. Visitors from countries other than the US, Canada and those in the EU will be expected to present an International Driver's Licence.

Local rate numbers: Avis 902 248 824, www.avis.es; Hertz 917 497 778, www.hertz.es; Europcar 902 503 010, www.europcar.es.

CLIMATE

As a general rule, late spring to early summer and late summer to early autumn are the best times for visiting most parts of Spain. This avoids the most oppressive heat, not to mention the crowds and high-season hotel rates. In winter, temperatures plummet in the high central plains.

Summer temperatures in the north are ideal for swimming and sunbathing, but expect rain any time in the northwest. At the height of summer (July–August) even the locals try to escape the dry, merciless heat of Madrid and the central plains; the southern and east coast areas can be uncomfortably humid.

For winter sun, head for the Canary Islands where temperatures rarely fall below a monthly average of 17°C (62°F). On the mainland, the south coast and parts of the central and southeastern coast are pleasantly mild all year, but swimming is not really an option in winter. Of course, winter is the season for skiing in the Pyrenees and Andalucía's Sierra Nevada.

CLOTHING

If you're heading for the south coast in the height of summer, pack loose cotton clothes and take sun hats and sunscreen. In April, May and October, you may need a light sweater for the evenings. From

November to March, you should enjoy shirt-sleeve sunshine during the day, but this can be interrupted by chill winds from the mountains, so take a warm jacket or sweater.

Winter visitors to Madrid and the central plains region will need to pack warm clothing. If you're heading for the northwest at any time, take waterproof gear.

Dress codes are very casual in most resorts, but tourists sporting resort wear in a big, sophisticated city such as Madrid or Barcelona may attract stares. The Spanish enjoy dressing up for an occasion, and it is as well to look smart if you are visiting a good restaurant or reputable nightclub. Short skirts, shorts and beachwear are considered inappropriate attire for visits to churches, so carry a wrap to cover bare arms and legs.

CRIME AND SAFETY

Spain's crime rate is on a par with the rest of Europe. Be on your guard against pickpockets and bag snatchers. Always carry a minimum of cash and keep your passport, travellers' cheques, credit cards and cash in a money belt or, better still, in your hotel safe. Never leave bags unattended, especially when swimming.

The most common crime against the tourist in Spain is theft from hire cars. If you park overnight in the street in one of the big towns or resorts, it's possible that your car will be broken into. Always look for secure parking areas and stow all possessions, especially video cameras and valuables, out of sight in the boot (trunk); never leave anything in your car overnight.

All thefts must be reported to the police within 24 hours. Go to the nearest police station *(comisaría)* and make a *denuncia*. You will need

---

I want to report a theft. **Quiero denunciar un robo.**
My handbag/ticket/wallet/passport has been stolen **Me han robado el bolso/el billete/la cartera/el pasaporte.**

a copy of the police report in order to make a claim on your holiday insurance. As a precaution, photocopy the relevant pages of your passport(s) and airline ticket(s) and keep them in a separate place from the originals. This will save much time in the event of them being stolen. If this happens your consulate should also be informed.

D

DISABLED TRAVELLERS

Facilities for travellers with disabilities are improving all the time, but as yet public transport is not fully wheelchair accessible. The Spanish National Tourist Office provides a fact sheet and a list of accessible accommodation. Most museums and other sights are wheelchair accessible. Visually impaired travellers can contact once, the Organización Nacional de Ciegos de España (Spanish National Organization for the Blind), Calle Sebastián Herrera 15, 28012 Madrid, tel: 915 068 888, www.once.es.

DRIVING

In Spain you drive on the right and overtake on the left. By law, drivers must have a valid driving licence, vehicle registration document and valid insurance documents, and must be able to show a passport or ID card.

Rules and regulations. Speed limits are 50kmh (30mph) in built-up areas, 90–100kmh (55–60mph) on main roads, and 120kmh (75mph) on motorways. The use of front and rear seat belts is obligatory. A red warning-triangle must be carried and you should display a nationality sticker. You must have a yellow reflective jacket in the front of the car to be used in case of roadside emergency. Motorcycle riders and their passengers must wear crash helmets. Don't drink and drive: the permitted blood-alcohol level is low, penalties are stiff and random breath tests are often carried out.

Roads are patrolled by the motorcycle police of the Civil Guard

(Guardia Civil). They can impose on-the-spot fines for minor offences, including speeding and travelling too close to the car in front.

Petrol stations. Service stations are plentiful, but keep an eye on the gauge in more remote areas. Unleaded petrol *(gasolina sin plomo)* comes in two grades, super and super-plus, and diesel *(gasóleo)* is widely available.

> Full tank, please, top grade. **Llénelo, por favor, con super.**
> Please check the oil/tyres/battery. **Por favor, controle el aceite/los neumáticos/la batería.**

Road signs. Most of the road signs used in Spain are international pictograms. Here are some written signs you will come across:

> **Autopista (de peaje)** (Toll) motorway (expressway)
> **Ceda el paso** Give way (Yield)
> **Circunvalación** Bypass/ring-road
> **Curva peligrosa** Dangerous bend
> **Despacio** Slow
> **Desviación** Diversion (Detour)
> **Obras** Road works
> **Peligro** Danger
> **Prohibido aparcar** No parking

Parking *(aparcamiento)*. Parking regulations are strictly enforced – offending vehicles will be towed away, and a hefty fine charged for their return. Some no parking signs have a large 'E' *(estacionamiento)* with a diagonal line through it. A yellow-painted kerb means parking is prohibited. Blue means parking is restricted to certain times and that you have to pay for and display a sticker, usually obtained from a nearby machine. These spaces are for a maximum of two hours. Parking is usually free on Sundays and public holidays. Underground car parks with a security attendant are the safest bet. **Breakdowns and assistance.** For emergencies dial 112. On motorways there are SOS boxes located at 2km (1 mile) intervals.

My car has broken down. **Mi coche se ha estropeado.** Where is the nearest garage? **¿Donde está el garage más cercano?**

E

ELECTRICITY

220V/50Hz AC is now standard. Sockets take round, two-pin plugs, so you may need an adapter.

EMBASSIES AND CONSULATES

All embassies (a selection of which are listed below) are in Madrid. Many countries have consular facilities in large cities, such as Barcelona and Seville, as well as in resort areas and islands popular with foreign tourists, such as the Costa del Sol, the Canary Islands and Palma, Mallorca. If you run into trouble with the authorities or the police, the embassy can advise you where to find the nearest consulate.

Australia Torre Espacio Paseo de la Castellana 259D, tel: 913 536 600; www.spain.embassy.gov.au.

Canada Torre Espacio Paseo de la Castellana 259D, tel: 913 828 400; www.canadainternational.gc.ca.

Ireland Paseo de la Castellana 46, tel: 914 364 093; www.irlanda.es.

South Africa Claudio Coello 91, tel: 914 363 780; www.dirco.gov.za/madrid/en.

UK Torre Espacio Paseo de la Castellana 259D, tel: 917 146 300; www.gov.uk/government/world/organisations/british-embassy-madrid.

US Serrano 75, tel: 915 872 200; http://madrid.usembassy.gov.

EMERGENCIES

Unless you are fluent in Spanish you should seek help through your hotel receptionist or the local tourist office. If you can speak Spanish, the following telephone numbers may be useful.

Fire Brigade 080 **Red Cross (Cruz Roja)** 902 222 292
Police 091 **Sea Rescue** 900 202 202
112 will connect you to Fire, Police or Ambulance.

G

GETTING THERE

By air from North America. Iberia (tel: 1 807 772 4642; www.iberia.com) has flights from New York City, Boston, Chicago and Miami to Madrid, and connections from there to Málaga, Seville and other smaller airports; Air Europa (tel: 1 800 238 7672, www.air-europa.com) has flights from New York City and from Miami (seasonal) to Madrid, and connections from there to Málaga, Seville and other smaller airports. It also has a weekly scheduled flight between New York City and Málaga, in each direction.

By air from Europe. Scheduled flights link major European cities directly to the most important cities, and charter flights arrive in their hundreds from numerous destinations in northern Europe.

By car. From the UK, the main route from the French ferry ports runs south through western France to Bordeaux and into Spain at Irún, west of the Pyrenees. Alternatively, take the more central route through France to Perpignan in the southeast, then you can follow the A7 motorway to Barcelona and other points south.

Driving time can be cut by using the long-distance car-ferry service from Plymouth to Santander and Portsmouth to Bilbao in northern Spain.

By rail. From the UK, take the high-speed Eurostar (www.eurostar.com) from London's St Pancras Station, through the Channel Tunnel to Paris Gare du Nord. French National Railways SNCF (www.voyages-sncf.com) and their Spanish compatriots RENFE now operate double-decker high-speed trains (TGV) from Paris Gare de Lyon to Figueres, Girona and Barcelona. You can now go from Paris to Barcelona centre to centre in around 6h15. There are usually two trains per day, four a day in summer. From either of those places take a Spanish train (www. renfe.es) to your destination.

By sea. From the UK, one company offers car ferry services to mainland Spain, with schedules varying by the season. Brittany Ferries (tel: 0871 244 0744, www.brittanyferries.com) has sailings with an average crossing time of 24 hours between Plymouth and Santander. There are also cruises to Spain (Bilbao, Santander) departing from Portsmouth.

H

HEALTH AND MEDICAL CARE

Anything other than basic emergency treatment can be very expensive, and you should not leave home without adequate insurance, preferably including cover for an emergency flight home in the event of serious injury or illness.

EU citizens are entitled to free emergency hospital treatment – you must obtain a European Health Insurance Card (ehic) before you leave. For information, tel: 0845 605 0707; apply online at www.ehic.org.uk or obtain an application form from the post office. You may have to pay part of the price of treatment or medicines; keep receipts so that you can claim a refund when you return home.

For minor ailments, visit the local first-aid post *(ambulatorio)*. *Farmacias* (chemist/drugstore) are usually open during normal shopping hours – a green cross on a white background signifies a chemist.

After hours, at least one chemist per town remains open all night; called a *farmacia de guardia*, its location is posted in the window of all other chemists and in the local newspapers.

One of the main health hazards is also Spain's biggest attraction – the sun. Take along a sun hat, sunglasses and plenty of sunscreen.

Where's the nearest (all-night) chemist? **¿Dónde está la farmacia (de guardia) más cercana?**
I need a doctor/dentist. **Necesito un médico/dentista.**
sunburn/sunstroke **quemadura del sol/una insolación**
an upset stomach **dolor de estómago**

L

LANGUAGE

The national language of Spain, Castilian Spanish *(castellano)*, is spoken throughout the country, but it is estimated that two out of every five Spaniards speak another language primarily. The inhabitants of the Basque Country, Galicia, Catalunya and the Valencia region and the Balearics speak Euskara, Gallego, Catalan and variants of Catalan, respectively.

English is widely spoken in the resort towns, though it is polite to learn at least a few basic phrases. The Berlitz Spanish Phrasebook and Dictionary covers most situations you are likely to encounter.

LOST PROPERTY

For items left behind on public transport, ask your hotel receptionist to telephone the bus or railway station or taxi company. If you still cannot find the missing item, report the loss to the Municipal Police or the Guardia Civil within 24 hours (see page 172). They will issue a form you will need if you wish to make an insurance claim once you are home.

M

MEDIA

Radio and television *(radio; televisión)*. Depending upon where you are it is possible, especially on the Costas and in the Canary Islands and parts of the Balearics, to find radio stations that broadcast in English on the FM band. Network television programmes are all in Spanish, but better hotels and many English bars also have satellite TV with CNN, MTV, Superchannel, Sky TV, etc.

Newspapers and magazines *(periódico, revista)*. In the major tourist areas you can buy most European newspapers on the day of publication, with some English ones even having Spanish editions, but at about three times the price. *The International Herald Tribune* is widely available, as are British and American magazines. In the Costas and the islands there are numerous weekly/monthly English-language newspapers and magazines, some of which are free.

MONEY

The monetary unit of Spain is the euro (e), with 100 cents making 1 euro. Banknotes are issued in denominations of 5, 10, 20, 50, 100, 200 and 500 euros. Coins in circulation are 1, 2, 5, 10, 20 and 50 cents. The euro is roughly equivalent to US$1.

Banks and currency exchange. Outside normal banking hours, many travel agencies and other businesses displaying a *cambio* sign will

Where's the nearest bank? **¿Dónde está el banco más cercano?**
I want to change some pounds/dollars. **Quiero cambiar libras/dólares.**
Do you take travellers' cheques? **¿Acceptan cheques de viaje?**
Can I pay with a credit card? **¿Se puede pagar con tarjeta?**

change foreign currency into euros. All larger hotels will also change guests' money, but the exchange rate is less favourable than at the bank. Travellers' cheques always get a better rate than cash. Always take your passport with you when you go to change money or travellers' cheques.

Cashpoints. ATMs outside banks are widely available in Spain, and are by far the easiest way of obtaining cash advances in euros, drawn on either your debit or credit card; they also provide a better exchange rate than cash or travellers' cheques. Check that your account and PIN number are authorised for international withdrawals.

Credit cards and travellers' cheques *(tarjetas de crédito; cheques de viaje)*. These are accepted in the majority of hotels, restaurants and big shops.

VAT (IVA). IVA *(impuesto sobre el valor añadido)*, value added tax, will be added to your hotel and restaurant bills; it currently stands at 21 percent (general rate for most services and products), 10 percent (reduced rate) and 4 percent for basic products such as milk and bread. Generally these prices are included in the advertised total, but do peruse the menu carefully beforehand to check. In the Canary Islands value added tax is known as IGIC and levied at a rate of 7 percent (general rate) on hotel rooms. If shops display a 'Tax Free Shopping' sign, EU residents can get a tax refund if they make a big purchase.

O

OPENING TIMES

Shops, offices and other businesses generally open Mon–Fri 9am to 5/5.30pm, but in tourist areas many places stay open all day. Most museums have also given up the habit to close for the siesta and usually remain open from 9am until 7pm. Some are closed on Monday. Banks generally open Monday to Friday 9.30am–2pm, and on Saturday 9.30am–1pm, but beware of the numerous public holidays.

P

POLICE

There are three separate police forces in Spain. The Policía Municipal or Local are attached to the local town hall and usually wear a blue uniform; they are the ones to whom you report theft and other crimes. The Policía Nacional is a national anti-crime unit whose officers wear a dark blue uniform, and the Guardia Civil, with green uniforms, is a national force whose most conspicuous role is to act as a highway patrol and customs officials. The emergency number is 112.

POST OFFICES

Post offices (www.correos.es) handle mail only. You cannot normally make telephone calls from them. Opening hours vary slightly between towns, but are generally Monday to Friday 8.30am–2.30pm, and on Saturday 9.30am–1pm. The post office at Barajas airport in Madrid also opens Sundays. Stamps (*sellos*) are also on sale at tobacconists (*estancos*) and hotel desks, and at tourist shops selling postcards. Mail for destinations outside Spain should be posted in the box marked *extranjero* (overseas). Allow about a week for delivery to the US and 4–5 days to the UK. To speed things up, send a letter *urgente* (express) or *certificado* (registered).

PUBLIC HOLIDAYS

Banks, post offices, government offices and many other businesses will be closed on the following national holidays. They may also shut on local and regional holidays; check with the local tourist office.

1 January *Año Nuevo* New Year's Day
6 January *Epifanía* Epiphany
March/April *Jueves Santo* Maundy Thursday; *Viernes Santo* Good Friday
1 May *Día del Trabajo* Labour Day/May Day
May/June *Corpus Christi* Corpus Christi

15 August *Asunción* Feast of the Assumption
12 October *Día de la Hispanidad* Columbus Day
1 November *Todos los Santos* All Saints' Day
6 December *Día de la Constitución* Constitution Day
8 December *Immaculada Concepción* Immaculate Conception
25 December *Día de Navidad* Christmas Day

PUBLIC TRANSPORT

Buses *(autobús)*. There are extensive bus services within and between major cities, but in the countryside services generally only
run to and from provincial centres – so links to smaller towns and
resorts may not be possible, even if they are quite close by. Buses
often go to destinations that are not served by trains, and are usually cheaper, faster and more frequent.

Where is the (nearest) bus stop? **¿Dónde está la parada de**
    autobuses (más cercana)?
When's the next bus/train for...? **¿A qué hora sale el próximo**
    autobús/tren para...?
I want a ticket to... **Quiero un billete para...**
single (one-way) **ida**
return (round-trip) **ida y vuelta**
Will you tell me when to get off? **¿Podría indicarme cuándo**
    tengo que bajar?

Trains *(tren)*. Madrid is the hub of the RENFE (Spanish National Railways) network, which reaches out like a spider's web to most corners
of the country. There is a bewildering number of different types of train
service, from all-stops local services *(cercanías)* to the high-speed AVE
that makes the trip from Madrid to Seville in just 2.5 hours.

Timetables and information are available from railway stations
and tourist offices, and from the RENFE website (www.renfe.es).

American visitors can take advantage of the Spain Eurail Pass, which allows 3–10 days of unlimited rail travel starting at US$252 (2nd class) or $314 (first class). The Spain Rail 'n' Drive Pass gives three days of unlimited rail travel plus two days of car hire. Prices depend on class of rail travel and car category and start at US$392 per person for two travelling together.

For information on further deals available, such as **Eurail** passes for UK visitors, and services including the high-speed Euromed (Barcelona, Valencia, Alicante) or AVE (Madrid, Córdoba, Seville, Cádiz, Málaga) trains, contact Rail Europe at www.raileurope.com or www.eurorailways.com. Both websites contain useful rail trip planning information, especially the section on 'Fares and Schedules'.

Taxis *(taxi)*. In the major cities, taxis have meters, but in smaller towns and villages they usually don't, so it's a good idea to check the fare before you get in. If you take a long trip, you will be charged a two-way fare whether you make the return journey or not. By law a taxi may carry only four passengers. A green light and/or a *libre* (free) sign indicates a taxi that is available.

Ferries *(barcos)*. These are a useful form of transport between the Canary and Balearic islands themselves and, to a lesser extent, to and from the islands. Trasmediterránea (www.trasmediterranea.es) is the largest company operating ferry services in Spain.

T

TELEPHONE

The country code for Spain is 34. All Spanish telephone numbers are 9-digit, and the number, which incorporates the area code, must be dialled in full – even for local calls.

There are phone booths in all major towns and cities from which you can make local and international calls. Instructions in English and dialling codes for different countries are displayed in the booths. Some telephones accept credit cards, and many require a phone card *(tar-*

jeta telefónica), available from *estancos*. To call abroad from Spain dial 00, then dial the country code, the area code (minus the initial 0) and the number. The country code for the US and Canada is 1; the UK 44; Australia 61; New Zealand 64; the Republic of Ireland 353; and South Africa 27.

Calling directly from your hotel room is almost always very expensive unless you use a calling card, or some other similar system, from your local long-distance supplier – in which case find out from the supplier the free connection number applicable to the country. They are different for each country and are not always easily available once you are there.

Another option is to use a private booth that advertises its prices for particular countries in the window or on boards outside. Their rates are highly competitive, and you pay on completion of the call.

Can you get me this number? **¿Puede comunicarme con este número?**

TIME ZONES

Spanish time is the same as that of most of Western Europe – Greenwich Mean Time plus one hour. In summer, another hour is added for Daylight Saving Time, keeping it an hour ahead of British Summer Time. The time in the Canary Islands is one hour earlier than on mainland Spain.

New York	London	**Spain**	Sydney	Auckland
6am	11am	**noon**	8pm	10pm

TIPPING

Since a service charge is normally included on hotel and restaurant bills, tipping is not obligatory but it's usual to leave a small coin on a bar counter, and 15 percent on restaurant bills. If you tip taxi drivers, 10 percent is enough unless they are especially helpful. Additional guidelines:

Hotel porter, per bag €1

Lavatory attendant €1

Tour guide €2

Hairdresser 10-15 percent

Maid €1 per day

TOILETS

The most commonly used expressions for toilets are *servicios* or *aseos*. Toilet doors are distinguished by *señoras* (ladies) or *damas* (women) and *caballeros* (men), and by pictograms.

Public conveniences are rare, but all hotels, bars and restaurants have toilets, usually of a reasonable standard, for the use of customers.

Where are the toilets? **¿Dónde están los servicios?**

TOURIST INFORMATION

There are Spanish National Tourist Offices in many countries. These include:

Canada 2 Bloor Street West, 34th Floor, Toronto 3402, Ontario M4W 3E2, tel: 416 961 4079, email: toronto@tourspain.es.

UK 6th floor, 64 North Row, W1K 7DE, London, W1W 6XB, tel: 0207 317 2011.

US Water Tower Place, Suite 915 East, 845 N. Michigan Avenue, Chicago, IL 60611, tel: 312-642 1992, email: chicago@tour spain.es; 8383 Wilshire Boulevard, Suite 960, Beverly Hills, Los Angeles, CA 90211, tel: 323 658 7195, email: losangeles@tour spain.es; 60 East 42nd Street - Suite 5300 (53rd Floor), New York, NY NY 10165-0039, tel: 212-265 8822, email: nuevayork@tourspain.es; 2655 Le Jeune

Rd (Gables International Plaza), Suite 605. Coral Gables, Miami, FL
33134, tel: 305-774 9643, email: miami@tourspain.es.
  For further information check the website www.spain.info.

Where is the tourist office? **¿Dónde está la oficina de turismo?**

V

VISAS AND ENTRY REQUIREMENTS

Most visitors, including citizens of EU countries, the US, Canada, Australia and New Zealand, require only a valid passport to enter Spain.
Nationals of countries that do not have a reciprocal agreement with
Spain need a visa. Visa requirements do change, so make sure to
check the situation with the Spanish Embassy in your country before
you leave.

Currency restrictions. Tourists may bring an unlimited amount
of currency in any form into the country, although amounts over
€10,000 must be declared.

W

WEBSITES

Spain's official tourism website is www.spain.info.
Some regional websites are as follows:
Andalucía including Costa del Sol: www.andalucia.org
Balearic Islands: http://www.illesbalears.travel/wwwib/index.html
Barcelona: www.barcelonaturisme.com
Basque Country: http://tourism.euskadi.eus/en
Canary Islands: www.holaislascanarias.com
Catalonia: www.catalunya.com
Madrid: www.turismomadrid.es, www.esmadrid.com
Valencia: www.comunitatvalenciana.com, www.turisvalencia.es

RECOMMENDED HOTELS

The following hotels and other types of accommodation in towns, cities and resorts throughout Spain are listed alphabetically. It is best to reserve well in advance, particularly if you will be visiting in the high season – which can vary from destination to destination and often coincides with important *fiestas*.

Prices do not normally include breakfast or iva, the 10 percent value added tax. The symbols are an approximate guide to indicate the price for a double room with bath or shower in the high season. Low season rates can be considerably lower. It is sometimes possible to negotiate special deals or weekend rates.

€€€€€	over 300 euros
€€€€	180–300 euros
€€€	120–180 euros
€€	90–120 euros
€	50–90 euros

AVILA

Palacio de los Velada €€ *Plaza de la Catedral, 10, tel: 920 255 100,* www.veladahoteles.com. In the heart of the city, just a few metres from the cathedral, this 16th-century palace has been carefully restored and converted into a beautiful hotel. Each of the 144 rooms is individually decorated. The restaurant boasts a spectacular courtyard.

BARCELONA

Astoria €€€€ *París 203, tel: 932 098 311,* www.hotelastoria.es. A member of the Derby hotel chain, this is a sophisticated and quiet establishment a few paces from prime shopping territory on Diagonal. Built in the 1950s, the Astoria has been refurbished and is very elegant. Some of the 144 rooms have small sitting rooms or garden terraces. Restaurant, bar and rooftop pool and terrace.

Condes de Barcelona €€€€€ *Passeig de Gracia 73, tel: 934 450 000*, www.condesdebarcelona.com. Just a block away from Gaudí's La Pedrera, this popular hotel occupies two former palaces. The 235 rooms are large, modern and elegant – ask for one with a Jacuzzi. A favourite of architects, designers, and European and Japanese tourists.

Mesón Castilla Atiram €€€ *Valldonzella 5, tel: 933 182 182*, www.atiramhotels.com. A quiet, dignified hotel with 60 rooms, located on the Plaça Castilla just 100m/yards or so from the Plaça Catalunya. Elegant public rooms and a private garage.

Sant Agustí €€ *Plaça Sant Agustí 3, tel: 933 181 658*, www.hotelsa.com. Supposedly the oldest hotel in the city, founded in 1840, in a pretty little square near La Rambla. 75 rooms.

Serhs Rivoli Ramblas €€€–€€€€ *La Rambla 128, tel: 933 481 7676*, www.hotelserhsrivolirambla.com. A busy townhouse hotel on La Rambla, with the never-ending parade just beyond the front door. Smallish, well-equipped, sound-proofed rooms have a combination of art deco and avant-garde style. Great views from the terrace, where there is also a fitness centre, sauna and solarium. 125 rooms.

Silken Gran Hotel Havana €€€–€€€€€ *Gran Via de les Corts Catalanes 647, tel: 933 417 000*, www.hoteles-silken.com. Founded in a charming house that dates from 1882, this was enlarged and turned into a deluxe hotel. It has an unusually shaped central atrium and a panoramic terrace with outdoor pool. The rooms and suites are modern and well-furnished. There is also 24-hour room service. 145 rooms.

BILBAO

López de Haro €€€–€€€€ *Obispo Oructa 2, tel: 944 235 500*, www.hotellopezdeharo.com. One of Bilbao's top hotels, located in a renovated 19th-century structure, combines a classical style with every latest facility. The hotel has 53 rooms, a champagne bar and a fine restaurant, and is situated in the city centre, close to the Guggenheim Museum.

CARMONA

Casa Palacio de Carmona €€€–€€€€ *Plaza de Lasso, tel: 954 191 000*, www.casadecarmona.com. A 16th-century palace lovingly renovated into a beautiful, hospitable, luxurious hotel. Every room is unique, and filled with handpicked antiques from Madrid, London and Paris. 33 rooms.

CÓRDOBA

NH Colection Amistad Córdoba €€€ *Plaza Maimónides 3, tel: 957 420 335*, www.nh-hotels.com. Located in the Jewish quarter close to the Mezquita, two 18th-century mansions, next to the old Moorish wall, have been combined and restored to form a fully modernised hotel in harmony with this historic city. 84 rooms.

COSTA DEL SOL

Kempinski Resort Hotel €€€€€ *Carretera de Cádiz Km 159, Playa El Padrón, Estepona, tel: 952 809 500*, www.kempinski.com. Most rooms in this architecturally interesting hotel have a sea view. Guests enjoy a marvellous subtropical garden, a 1km (0.6 mile) -long beach, several pools, watersports and horse-riding facilities, an haute-cuisine restaurant and the Spa and Wellness centre. 149 rooms.

Roc Lago Rojo €€€ *Miami 5, La Carihuela, Torremolinos, tel: 952 387 666*, www.roc-hotels.com. Just 2km (1 mile) from the centre of Torremolinos and 25m from La Carihuela beach, this is a charming modern hotel with 144 rooms and good facilities.

GRANADA

Alhambra Palace €€€ *Plaza Arquitecto García de Paredes 1, tel: 958 221 468*, www.h-alhambrapalace.es. Impressive Moorish-style palace on the edge of the hill on which stands the Alhambra (five minutes' walk away), with stunning views across the city to the Sierra Nevada. 126 rooms.

Palacio de Santa Inés €–€€ *Cuesta de Santa Inés 9, tel: 958 222 362,* www.palaciosantaines.com. The 16th-century palace known as the House of the Eternal Father has been beautifully converted into a hotel of considerable charm. It is located in the historic Albaicín area, on the opposite bank of the Darro from the towering Alhambra fortress. 35 rooms.

LEÓN

Parador de León €€€€ *Plaza de San Marcos 7, tel: 987 237 300,* www. parador.es. Housed in an amazingly decorative 16th-century former convent, with an impressive Spanish Renaissance facade, this is one of Spain's finest and most luxurious *paradores*, as well as being a national monument. Ask for a room in the atmospheric old part, with its tapestry-lined walls. 226 rooms.

MADRID

Arosa €€€ *Calle de la Salud 21, tel: 915 321 600,* www.hotelarosa. com. Centrally located, just off the Gran Vía and not far from the Puerta del Sol. Rooms range from the grand old style of the original building to sleek, modern quarters, some decorated in Japanese-style. Swimming pool. 126 rooms.

Hesperia Madrid €€€–€€€€ *Paseo de la Castellana 57, tel: 912 108 800,* www.hesperia-madrid.com. A modern contemporary-style hotel, the first of its kind in Madrid. Expect to find distinguished rooms and public areas, exemplary service and fine restaurants. 170 rooms.

Room Mate Mario €€–€€€ *Campomanes 4, tel: 915 488 548,* www. room-matehotels.com. Situated in the historic centre of the city, close to the Opera, the Royal Palace, and the Gran Vía, this is a modern hotel decorated in a strikingly minimalist style with beautiful lighting and original bathrooms. 54 rooms.

Santo Domingo €€€–€€€€ *Plaza de Santa Domingo 13, tel: 915 479 800,* www.hotelsantodomingo.com. A hotel museum in a quiet location not far from the Puerta del Sol with its own collection of antiques, paintings and works of art. Each of the 120 rooms is different in style and decor from the others.

Wellington €€€€–€€€€€ *Velázquez 8, tel: 915 754 400*, www.hotel-wellington.com. Stylish hotel close to the Prado and the Puerta de Alcalá. All rooms have a classical decor combined with the latest in facilities. Fine restaurant and nice bar, too. 262 rooms.

MÉRIDA

Parador de Mérida €€€ *Plaza de la Constitución 3, tel: 924 313 800*, www.parador.es. Located in what was once an 18th-century convent that, itself, was on the site of a Roman Praetorian Guard palace. An elegant mix of history and style. 81 rooms.

PAMPLONA

Avenida €–€€€ *Avenida de Zaragoza 5, tel: 948 245 454*, www.avenida hotel.es. Has an unusual wedge-shaped facade, and the balconies of this restored building overlook the fountain on Plaza Príncipe de Viana. The 24 rooms are comfortable but small. Prices increase significantly for two weeks in July during San Fermín.

SALAMANCA

Rector €€€–€€€€ *Paseo del Rector Esperabe 10, tel: 923 218 482*, www.hotelrector.com. This magnificent building, once home to one of Salamanca's most aristocratic families, has been tastefully converted into a delightful small hotel. 13 rooms.

SAN SEBASTIÁN

La Galería €€–€€€ *Infanta Cristina 1–3, tel: 943 317 559*, www. hotel lagaleria.com. Handsome French-style 1890s house with individually decorated rooms. Situated not far from Ondarreta beach and the

Palacio de Miramar, and close to San Sebastián's shops and *tapas* bars. 23 rooms. Special offers with golf packages.

María Cristina €€€€–€€€€€ *Paseo República Argentina, 4, tel: 943 437 600,* www.starwoodhotels.com. A grand belle époque building dating from 1912 that used to be King Alfonso XIII's winter headquarters. Modern facilities and extra luxuries make it the finest hotel in San Sebastián. 139 rooms with views of either the city or the river.

SANTIAGO DE COMPOSTELA

Hostal Dos Reis Católicos €€€€–€€€€€ *Plaza do Obradoiro 1, tel: 981 582 200,* www.parador.es. Built by the Catholic Monarchs in the late 15th century, and expanded in the 17th and 18th centuries, this is Spain's most famous *parador* and reputedly the world's oldest hotel. Located on a magnificent square, the *parador* combines history with modern facilities. 136 rooms.

SEGOVIA

Exe casa de Los Linajes €–€€ *Dr Velasco 9, tel: 921 460 475,* www.exe casadeloslinajes.com. Just a two-minute walk from the Plaza Mayor, the hotel occupies a 17th-century building located on the edge of the old city, overlooking the countryside. Most of the 55 rooms have a terrace.

SEVILLE

Alfonso XIII €€€€€ *San Fernando 2, tel: 954 917 000,* www.hotel-alfonsoxiii-sevilla.com. Opened by King Alfonso XIII in 1929, this imposing hotel in the city centre is set in its own lovely gardens and epitomises Sevillian style and luxury. The spacious rooms are classically decorated and the lobby bar is a meeting point for Seville's high society. 147 rooms.

Doña Maria €€€ *Don Remondo 19, tel: 954 224 990,* www.hdmaria.com. A charming hotel with an interesting mix of antiques and modern facilities, plus a rooftop pool and bar. Excellent central location, almost within touching distance of the Giralda and cathedral. 70 rooms.

Los Seises by Fontecruz €€€€ *Segovias 6, tel: 954 229 495,* www.fontecruzhoteles.com. A 16th-century palace where historic surroundings combine with modern facilities to create an intriguing ambiance. Located in the Barrio de Santa Cruz, it has a rooftop pool overlooking the nearby cathedral and Giralda. 42 rooms.

Simón €€ *García de Vinuesa 19, tel: 954 226 660,* www.hotelsimonsevilla.com. A handsome hotel with 31 rooms in a renovated 18th-century townhouse, across from the cathedral. Has a lovely central courtyard around a small fountain.

TOLEDO

Parador de Toledo €€€ *Cerro del Emperador s/n, tel: 925 221 850,* www.parador.es. Seventy-seven comfortable rooms, a fine restaurant, traditional service and a pool – plus magnificent views over Toledo.

Pintor El Greco €€ *Alamillos del Tránsito 13, tel: 925 285 191,* www.hotelpintorelgreco.com. Delightful 17th-century house, with 33 pleasant rooms, modern comforts and car parking. Located in a charming section of the old Jewish quarter close to most monuments.

VALENCIA

Ayre Hotel Astoria Palace €€€–€€€€ *Plaza de Rodrigo Botet 5, tel: 96 398 10 00,* www.ayrehoteles.com. Located in the city centre, the Astoria Palace is a big, luxurious and impeccably renovated hotel with a range of English-style decorated rooms. Facilities include a fitness centre, a restaurant and a bar. 172 rooms.

THE BALEARIC ISLANDS

IBIZA

Ca'spla €€€–€€€€ *San Miguel de Balanzat, tel: 971 334 587,* www.caspla-ibiza.com. Listed as a 'Hotel Rural' this is at least as good as any 5-star hotel. Large and eclectically decorated rooms (some even with a private pool) are set in luxuriant grounds with wooden-beamed patios overlooking the pool. 16 rooms.

Club Cala Moli €€ *Apartado 105, San Josep, tel: 971 806 002,* www.calamoli.com. Located in the quieter southeastern part of the island, this is a charming *hostal* with attractive views from the pool and patio out over the Mediterranean. 10 rooms.

Hacienda Na Xamena €€€€–€€€€€ *Urb. Na Xamena s/n, San Miguel de Balanzat, tel: 971 334 500,* www.hotelhacienda-ibiza.com. Perched dramatically on high cliffs, overlooking the Mediterranean, this luxury hotel has the finest location on Ibiza. The decor is an intriguing mix of traditional Ibicenco style and art deco. 65 rooms.

MALLORCA

Barceló Formentor €€€€–€€€€€ *Playa de Formentor, Port de Pollença, tel: 971 899 100,* www.barcelo.com. In a fantastic location, possibly the best in the Balearics, surrounded by forests and with sculpted gardens leading onto a beautiful bay surrounded by mountains. A classical, formal hotel often frequented by famous personalities. Four restaurants and a health and beauty centre. 250 rooms.

Convent de la Missió €€€€ *Carrer de la Missió 7a, Palma de Mallorca, tel: 971 227 347,* www.conventdelamissio.com. This stylish hotel, in a converted 17th-century convent in the old quarter, has light, airy rooms, a roof terrace, sauna and an excellent restaurant. There is an art gallery in the refectory. 14 rooms.

Es Molí €€€€€ *Carretera Valldemossa-Deià s/n, Deià, tel: 971 639 000,* www.esmoli.com. An elegant hotel in a converted 19th-century manor house on a hill just outside Deià, with incomparable views of the village and sea. The pool is spring-fed, and the hotel is set in 15,000 sq m (18,000 sq yd) of gardens. The service is splendid. Breakfast on the terrace. The highly recommended restaurant, Ca'n Quet (open only for private functions), has its own garden. Closed November to mid-April. 87 rooms.

MENORCA

Del Almirante €€ *Carretera Maó-Es Castell, Es Castells, tel: 971 362 700*, www.hoteldelalmirante.com. Family-run hotel in an 18th-century English mansion overlooking Mahon harbour. It used to be the house of the Admiral Collingwood, Nelson's right-hand man and it is beautifully decorated with antiques and period pictures. 39 rooms.

Port Mahón €€€–€€€€ *Av. Port de Maó, s/n, Mahón, tel: 971 362 600*, www.sethotels.com. A charming hotel with an attractive facade, and gardens with a pool, overlooking the wide expanse of the Mahón harbour. Good size rooms, especially those with balconies overlooking the water. Swimming pool. 82 rooms.

THE CANARY ISLANDS

FUERTEVENTURA

Riu Palace Tres Islas €€–€€€ *Grandes Playas, Corralejo, tel: 928 535 700*, www.riu.com. Perfectly located on the magnificent beach, with a view of the dunes and Lanzarote. Very well appointed rooms, attractive pool and terrace, and nightly entertainment in the piano bar and Betancuria lounge. 401 rooms.

GRAN CANARIA

Las Calas €€ *El Arenal, 36 La Lechuza, Vega de San Mateo, tel: 630 968 679*, www.hotelrurallascalas.com. A friendly old farmhouse converted into a small, relaxed boutique hotel high in the Gran Canaria countryside. Typical home-cooked Canarian food is served in the intimate dining room. 9 rooms.

Puerto de Mogán €€–€€€ *Urbanización Puerto de Mogán s/n, Playa de Mogán, tel: 928 565 066*, www.hotelpuertodemogan.com. Enjoys a wonderful location at the end of the harbour in this delightful marina. Pleasant rooms with all the expected facilities, plus pool and bar, and swimming in the harbour. 56 rooms.

LA GOMERA

Jardín Tecina €€€–€€€€ *Lomada de Tecina, Playa de Santiago, tel: 922 145 850,* www.jardin-tecina.com. A stylish complex set in its own extensive gardens on the cliffs. The hotel has an array of restaurants, bars, pools, sports facilities and its own beach club. 434 rooms.

LA PALMA

Parador de la Palma €€€ *El Zumacal, Breña Baja, tel: 922 435 828,* www.parador.es. A *parador* located on the cliffs just to the south of, and overlooking, Santa Cruz. Traditionally Canarian in style and decor, it has 76 rooms.

LANZAROTE

Meliá Salinas €€€€€ *Avenida Islas Canarias, Costa Teguise, tel: 928 590 040,* www.melia.com. The island's largest and most luxurious hotel, and an integral part of the cultural heritage of Lanzarote. The stunning double atrium is filled with magnificent indoor gardens and waterfalls – the creations, as is the pool, of César Manrique. 309 rooms. For adults only.

TENERIFE

Bahia del Duque €€€€ *Avenida de Bruselas s/n, Playa de las Americas, Costa Adeje, tel: 922 746 932,* www.bahia-duque.com. An eclectic array of buildings set around a sub-tropical garden with pools, restaurants and bars that descend, over several levels, down to the beach. Traditionally dressed staff and peacocks roaming free. 362 rooms.

San Roque €€€–€€€€€ *Carretera Esteban de Ponte 32, Garachico, Isla Baja, tel: 922 133 435,* www.hotelsanroque.com. A beguiling and eclectic mix of a traditional 17th-century palace with wooden beamed ceilings and balconies, and modern art deco. The pool is set in a charming patio. 20 rooms.

INDEX

Berlitz POCKET GUIDE

SPAIN

Sixth Edition 2016

Editor: Carine Tracanelli
Authors: Emma Stanford, Nick Inman
Head of Production: Rebeka Davies
Picture Editor: Tom Smyth
Cartography Update: Carte
Update Production: AM Services
Photography Credits: Corbis 22; Corrie
Wingate/Apa Publications 4TC, 4MC, 4ML,
4TL, 5T, 5TC, 5MC, 5MC, 6TL, 6MC, 6TL, 6ML,
7M, 7T, 7T, 8L, 8R, 9, 9R, 10, 13, 15, 17, 18, 23,
28, 30, 31, 32, 35, 36, 39, 41, 43, 45, 46, 49, 51,
55, 56, 58, 60, 62, 67, 68, 70, 74, 78, 81, 82, 85,
87, 89, 91, 93, 94, 95, 96, 112, 115, 134, 137,
138, 143, 145, 146, 148; Deamstime 77, 105,
107, 111, 125; Fotolia 98; Getty Images 26,
108, 132; Greg Gladman/Apa Publications
7MC, 120, 121, 122; Gregory Wrona/Apa
Publications 5M;iStock 52, 64, 75, 99, 100,
110, 116, 124, 127, 129, 131; Kevin Jones/Apa
Publications 102, 119; Public domain 5M, 24;
Shutterstock 20, 72, 128
Cover Picture: AWL Images

Distribution
UK, Ireland and Europe: Apa Publications
(UK) Ltd; sales@insightguides.com
United States and Canada: Ingram Publisher
Services; ips@ingramcontent.com
Australia and New Zealand: Woodslane;
info@woodslane.com.au
Southeast Asia: Apa Publications (SN) Pte;
singaporeoffice@insightguides.com

Hong Kong, Taiwan and China:
Apa Publications (HK) Ltd;
hongkongoffice@insightguides.com
Worldwide: Apa Publications (UK) Ltd;
sales@insightguides.com

Contact us
Every effort has been made to provide
accurate information in this publication,
but changes are inevitable. The publisher
cannot be responsible for any resulting loss,
inconvenience or injury. We would appreciate
it if readers would call our attention to any
errors or outdated information. We also
welcome your suggestions; please contact us
at: berlitz@apaguide.co.uk
www.insightguides.com/berlitz

Berlitz®

speaking your language

phrase book & dictionary
phrase book & CD

Available in: Arabic, Brazilian Portuguese*, Burmese*, Cantonese
Chinese, Croatian, Czech*, Danish*, Dutch, English, Filipino, Finnish*, French,
German, Greek, Hebrew*, Hindi*, Hungarian*, Indonesian, Italian, Japanese,
Korean, Latin American Spanish, Malay, Mandarin Chinese, Mexican Spanish,
Norwegian, Polish, Portuguese, Romanian*, Russian, Spanish, Swedish, Thai,
Turkish, Vietnamese
*Book only